# HOW TO MANAGE
## BY *OBJECTIVES*

*John W. Humble*

# HOW TO
# MANAGE BY
# *OBJECTIVES*

---

A Division of American Management Associations

INTERNATIONAL STANDARD BOOK NUMBER: 0–8144–5322–8
Library of Congress catalog card number: 73–75671

FIRST PRINTING

Parts One and Two were originally published by Management Publications Limited, England, under the title *Management by Objectives.* Part One is based, with permission, on an article by the author published in *European Business,* Autumn 1970.

# PREFACE

No one denies that management by objectives has made a major contribution to better management in the past fifteen years. But at the same time no one doubts the wrong emphases and poor perceptions which have led to disappointments and failures. It is timely to see what common pattern of mistakes has emerged in the United States and elsewhere so that we may profit from our mistakes. That is what this book is all about.

Acknowledgments alone might fill a book. The debt I owe to Peter Drucker and Douglas McGregor is inestimable. When anyone asks for a reading list, I usually reply, "Read Drucker's *Practice of Management* and McGregor's *Human Side of Enterprise.* You'll find all the wisdom, stimulus, and originality about MBO expressed with the simplicity only great men can afford."

Without the encouragement of our clients, my colleagues and I in Urwick, Orr & Partners Ltd. would not be in a position to codify this practical experience. Peter Hives, who has special responsibilities for MBO in the Urwick Group, has made a major contribution to concepts and methods for many years.

The trouble with writing a book in a field full of change, experiment, and expansion is that one must freeze one's current prejudices at a certain moment in time. Within months the need to rewrite is painfully clear. I can only say that this book is a personal contribution to the continuing study of how to manage by objectives, not a final answer.

JOHN W. HUMBLE

*London and New York*

# CONTENTS

*Part One*

---

# THE PITFALLS OF MBO AND HOW TO AVOID THEM

Although the use of management by objectives is accelerating worldwide, some critics are finding fault with the system. Indeed, a minority of managers feel disillusioned by the MBO approach, and a recent research report by Walter Wikstrom of The Conference Board specifically states that companies with limited objectives for MBO, such as improving appraisal or as a basis for compensation decisions, have a fairly dismal record.

The problems, however, are not with the system itself, but with the incomplete or faulty application of it. As Wikstrom concludes:

> Some organizations have adopted MBO as a basic management philosophy and have followed the principles wherever they might lead. They led to changes in job assignments and reporting relationships, changes in the ways in which decisions are taken and in the men who are involved in the decision process, changes in the availability of information throughout the structure, and changes in the spirit of the employee group at all levels. This approach to MBO has proven to be

fantastically difficult, time consuming, frustrating . . . and valuable. The firms that have followed this approach are the ones that claim to see the results in improved performance by individuals, departments, divisions, and the total corporation.[1]

In this section I will try to suggest some ways of avoiding the common pitfalls of MBO which impede the development of this total approach.

### WHAT IS MBO?

Since new definitions proliferate daily, we should return to the original text. The term *management by objectives* was first used by Peter Drucker back in 1954, when he wrote:

> What the business enterprise needs is a principle of management that will give full scope to individual strength and responsibility and at the same time give common direction of vision and effort, establish teamwork, and harmonize the goals of the individual with the common weal. The only principle that can do this is Management by Objectives and self-control.[2]

In the 19 years that have passed since Drucker wrote these words, we have got into substantial difficulties when we have strayed from the broader implications of this definition. *At its best, management by objectives is a system that integrates the company's goals of profit and growth with the manager's needs to contribute and develop himself personally.* It is not a new wonder tool that can replace intelligent or sensitive leadership, and its misuse can cause more harm than good.

4

Harry Levinson points out one of the major potential pitfalls of MBO. It fails, he says, to take into account the deeper emotional roots of a manager's motivation. The MBO process puts the manager in the same position as the rat in a psychologist's laboratory maze. The rat performs in a certain way to get the food; if he fails to perform, the experimenter starves the rat until he wants the food and learns to perform correctly. Says Harry Levinson:

> Management by objectives differs only in that it permits the man himself to determine his own bait from a limited range of choices. Having done so, the MBO process assumes that he will (a) work hard to get it, (b) be pushed internally by reason of his commitment, and (c) make himself responsible to his organization for doing so. In fairness to most managers, they certainly try, but not without increasing resentment and complaint for feeling like rats in a maze, guilt for not paying attention to those parts of the job not in their objectives, and passive resistance to the mounting pressure for ever-higher goals.[3]

Levinson's criticisms are valid for narrowly conceived MBO programs, but not for the all-pervasive MBO approach with which we are concerned.

### THE MANAGER'S SECRET PERSONAL GOALS

Although management is only too ready to try to define the goals of the company, it often ignores the deeply held personal goals of the manager himself. If the system is going to be management by objectives, some of them had better be *his* objectives. What does he want to do with his life? Where does he want to go? What

5

will make him feel good about himself? What does he want to be able to look back on when he has expended his unrecoverable years?

Some feel that these are personal questions that have nothing to do with business. But that is a serious delusion, and any MBO system that does not concern itself with the answers to these questions will be heading toward failure.

The renewed concern with human values in a way completes a 15-year cycle in the maturing of MBO. During the early years the leadership came from personnel men who saw MBO merely as a vehicle for improved communications and better training and development. As the limitations of this narrow approach became evident, the practice of MBO began to emphasize the clarification of total business objectives, the complexity of planning and control systems, the mechanics of integrating an overall management system. The perceptions of the behavioral scientists were studied and built unobtrusively into the best programs, but some MBO projects became overmechanistic. The current emphasis on the manager—his personal needs as an individual and his self-expression as a group member—is partly a reaction against this. It is also a reflection of the changing social scene and the different values and expectations people have in the 1970s.

### A BEHAVIORAL VIEW OF MBO

If we understand that MBO is both a planning and control system *and* a powerful agent of behavioral change and organization development, it can be seen as a "learning together" process in which human needs and values are as deeply involved as physical and financial factors. It must be admitted frankly that not all MBO programs have recognized this. However, the best ones have persistently sought to put proven behavioral research into action.

MBO is, in a sense, a sincere attempt to demonstrate the reality of McGregor's Theory Y. When MBO work starts, we assume that most people will direct and control themselves willingly if they have shared in setting their own objectives. Because goals are pertinent to the individual, every manager is stimulated to seek improvement. The volume of good ideas which ensue vindicates the belief that there is a vast reservoir of untapped creativity and intellect. Of course, participation and personal clarity of purpose are not the only prerequisites of effective performance. Congruence of goals of various individuals is necessary to promote collaboration rather than rivalry.

The manager's job can be enriched in a number of ways. When the structure, key tasks, and decision points are analyzed critically by the managers themselves, organization change is inevitable: the number of levels is often reduced, and whole jobs are created with evident accountability.

In addition, a manager and his boss may meet regularly to appraise progress and problems, sitting down together to debate constructively objectives, controls, standards, and improvement ideas.

Participation is inherent in MBO done well, but the full complexity of this subject has to be explored further. In practical terms there can be participation at every stage—defining a problem, securing information, making a decision and executing it. Yet full participation at each of these stages may not always be appropriate.

7

*Exhibit 1.*

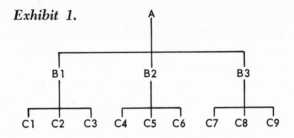

*Exhibit 2.*

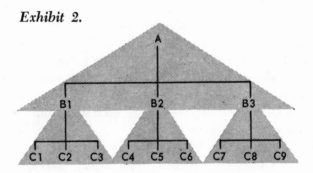

Exhibit 1 outlines a simple organizational structure. Exhibit 2 shows how these levels relate to each
other in the MBO approach. A will bring together his
B colleagues, brief them on MBO, and discuss its implications. Each B, with the adviser's help, will clarify
his key tasks and standards and look for improvement,
which he will discuss with A. After these personal discussions, A will meet again with all his B's to talk over
the common difficulties, cross-linking standards, con-
tradictory standards, and so on. Each B will repeat this
process with *his* people, who will in turn brief at D
level.

Obviously this method owes a great deal to the
work of Rensis Likert. It is an attempt to develop
the organization climate or culture; it clarifies crucial

boundary management problems and it helps to overcome problems of rigidity and obsolescence in organization structure.

The key executive group meets to review and discuss strategy. In the meantime, an adviser feeds back objective observations of the problem-solving methods and interpersonal skills being demonstrated, both of which contribute to overall group effectiveness.

A problem is exposed which cuts across the hierarchy: a task force is set up with clear objectives and a membership of those who have a knowledge to contribute. Status has no significance. The group is encouraged to marshal its resources and restructure according to the current problem. They may again be coached in effective teamwork.

A manager brings together his own subordinates to thrash out common problems and difficulties which affect them all.

All this is *teamwork*.

Businessmen generally are only just beginning to accept that the behavioral scientist has knowledge and insights of profound, practical value. The scientists also have a major learning problem in transferring their laboratory and research findings into an ongoing business. The exciting thing is that the partnership is being established.

It is important to keep perspective: commitment, motivation, and teamwork *are* important, but they complement disciplined systems for organization planning and control. One without the other means failure. Moreover, it is proper that businessmen should be critical before going wholeheartedly for a specific behavioral technique. For example, there is disquiet in some academic circles about the claims made for sensitivity

9

training in terms of "unfreezing" attitudes. George Odiorne, having summarized research by Argyris and Boss, concluded:

> Neither of these evaluations shows anything about *behavior* change on the job, nor do the 51 books, 68 articles, and 7 pamphlets on the subject published in other organizations. After 13 years or more of laboratory training then, research finds that not a single bit of proof exists in published form that laboratory training changes behavior.[4]

He has some powerful comments to make also on the problems of motivation training. My advice to any businessman would be to listen carefully to the behavioral scientist with in-depth business practice, read Odiorne—and then make up his own mind!

The important point is that our real concern is not to change attitudes but to change behavior. After all, attitudes are inferences from behavior, just as intelligence is. We cannot observe them directly. They seem to be acquired as a result of experience of the consequences of previous behavior. An individual who is generally successful in what he does is likely to become self-confident and look on the bright side of things. Attitudes do not have a one-to-one relationship with behavior, however. Performance depends just as much upon the environment in which the job is done. *Over*-concentration upon attitude change, as opposed to behavior change, leads to the neglect of more obvious ways to remove obstacles.

Thus, although behavior change may be facilitated by formal learning experience, it is perfectly possible to loosen up relationships and to encourage frankness previously absent by planned on-the-job methods. For example: get the man to clarify his tasks and commit himself to new challenges of a meaningful kind in a certain time. Have him participate with his boss in doing this. Let him work with his colleagues in teams and task forces where there is a common problem to solve. Let these task forces be helped to acquire skills of working effectively as a group by practical methods that don't expose all their personal fears and motives. Let the man and his colleagues build on their strengths and successes.

### INTRODUCING MBO INTO A BUSINESS

Even when all these factors have been fully understood, MBO programs can fail to live up to expectations. Very often this is because they were not introduced with the full support and understanding of the top management group. Indeed, management by objectives *must* involve all the executive managers of a company in a very direct way. Not only must they be involved in defining and rethinking their own objectives and the strategic purpose of the business, but they must also be receptive to comments, criticisms, and suggestions from their subordinates.

Any attempt to introduce management by objectives unobtrusively—for example, using it as only a part of a management development program—is doomed to failure.

When General Mills introduced an objectives-based performance appraisal program in 1954, its initiative lay mainly with the corporate personnel staff and its orientation was to personal development. Executive managers realized that individual improvement goals were unrelated to the overall business objectives and therefore not really meaningful.

After six years, the program was dropped, and a new MBO approach was developed by the top executives themselves. They saw MBO primarily as a valuable way to improve results through integrated planning and control. Personnel growth and development is a valuable by-product since General Mills now regards MBO not so much as a program as an approach to managing.

The senior management team should not approach MBO blissfully unaware of its demands on them. They should expect to attend briefing seminars, do some background reading, visit companies experienced in introducing MBO, and thoroughly understand what the program will involve.

Furthermore, it is unrealistic to believe that there is only *one* way to introduce management by objectives into a company. So much depends on the present situation. If, for example, a creative strategic plan, supported by operational plans covering even unit levels, already exists, it is possible to move in at unit level. Management by objectives can be used primarily as a tool to get these objectives into action through individual managers and teams of managers. On the other hand, a first stage of management by objectives can also be adopted primarily to diagnose whether the organization structure is effective.

To minimize problems, a large organization often does pilot work before launching a total companywide program. Thus a group of high-quality advisers can be trained and a tailor-made program drawn up to suit the special needs of the business. Once the pilot work has proved successful, a major effort is required to get MBO used throughout the entire business. Too many pilot exercises have remained just "interesting experiments."

However, management by objectives should never be introduced horizontally at a single level of management. For example, the attempt to apply management by objectives at supervisor level alone is certain to fail. The ideal sequence is usually for the board to clear its mind on company objectives and then communicate them down the line. The disadvantage, though, is that the board cannot make its best decisions in isolation and the ideas and perceptions of managers must be tapped and communicated up to the board. When this dialogue is carried out sincerely, both parties learn from one another.

Clearly the MBO work is not complete until it has embraced the full range of objectives from top to bottom of the business. Perhaps it still needs to be said, again and again, that MBO is concerned with the totality of the business and its results. Functions and departments are cost centers and improving their *efficiency* by no means guarantees the improved *effectiveness* of the total business. And, of course, MBO insists that the business must not be introspective. It must see that success, indeed existence, depends on perceiving sensitively the changing needs of its market and the society of which it is a part.

However, in practice, to insist that *nothing* can be done unless the main board itself completes its strategy may sometimes be naive. It can happen that operational managers are so heavily loaded with day-to-day work that they literally do not have the time to think ahead. Some crude work in setting unit objectives and in improving the performance of individual managers at a nonstrategic level may be a necessary starting point.

When managers start showing signs of improvement, more time and better control over their immediate problems should result. It is then possible to do some really worthwhile work for the future. This short-term effort, moreover, is also a training and educational period. Later, when a company's strategic goals are well expressed, they can be communicated to a group of managers who already understand how to define their own objectives and who are committed to change. In this way, the process of planning, control, and personal development becomes much more self-sustaining.

Consider this example of a launching sequence.

When J. Gulliver took over as chief executive of Fine Fare, a major British supermarket group, the company's profit record was poor with no trend toward improvement. Policies and objectives were ill defined. Control of the 320 supermarkets was overcentralized, staff morale was poor, and labor turnover high.

The first action taken was to review the company's strategy: each business sector was required to meet set financial criteria, unprofitable assets were pruned, and working capital and cash flow policies were established. Marketing policies were also reviewed and a manpower audit made. This alone saved the group $240,000. With strategy clear, Lynn Owen, director of trading operations, set out primary objectives:

☐ To stop current trading loss position during the first six months and during the second six months to reach break-even. This required a 10 percent increase in current gross sales turnover while maintaining gross profit margins.

☐ To improve staff morale and weld its members into a team.

Detailed MBO methods were then used to express these objectives right down the line. A pilot project in one store led to a 65 percent sales increase in six months; all stores then adopted the method. Every manager has a job performance target sheet, and in addition to normal management review, there are four program review meetings each year.

Thus, at Fine Fare, MBO started with a fundamental review of corporate strategy and the establishment of primary objectives. These were expressed through an improved organization structure with the *involvement and development of all the managers.* This work in four years increased Fine Fare sales from $180 million to $352 million; reversed "no profits" into $11.4 million profits; changed the return on capital invested from nil to 31 percent, and developed a management team with the will to continue this total strategy through the seventies.

### SACRIFICING MEN WHO CANNOT BE SPARED

Another pitfall managements fall into is thinking that the MBO program will take care of itself. Most successful management by objectives programs have required an adviser or team of advisers in order to help executive managers get the project moving.

If the adviser is of the highest quality and is respected within the company, then top management has done more to convey its *real* belief in the program than any formal written communication or presentation at a meeting. Willingness to sacrifice the time of a man who "cannot be spared" is the best testimony of the seriousness of intent of top management.

The adviser must be very thoroughly trained, since

he has two critical roles to play. *He must communicate the growing body of knowledge about the techniques, methods, and know-how of management by objectives to managers.* This is an educational role. And he must *facilitate changes in the relationships between people* and help to establish a constructive climate of opinion for success. This is a social role, in which the adviser is acting as a change agent.

The outside MBO consultant can help in two important ways. First, he can train the in-company advisers and counsel them in their early work. Second, he can act as a catalyst to the board itself and in the dialogue between the president or managing director and his immediate subordinates.

In relation to in-company advisers, the main problem, apart from selecting the wrong type of man, is the adviser who becomes overenthusiastic and does too much work personally, or who becomes mechanistic in issuing forms and procedures inherited from another company or from a textbook. Advisers should normally be seen as people who launch a program, and the justification for continuing the appointment, even in a large group, must be most carefully considered. Lasting success arises when the work is so built into the normal process of executive management that little or no specialist support is required.

D. K. Van Houten, General Manager of KLM, Royal Dutch Airlines, which introduced MBO into its worldwide field organization (with a workforce of 13,-000 people operating in 70 countries), points out that the adviser's "catalyst role is of great importance in helping managers to make this fresh appraisal of their objectives and their performance. It follows that the people assigned to this work, whether from inside or outside the business, must be of high quality and maturity and thoroughly trained in the latest techniques." The adviser must secure the positive participation of line management at every stage. As Mr. Van Houten concludes, "Attitudes cannot just be changed overnight and time, patience, and persistent counseling may be necessary if lasting benefit is to be obtained." This comment underlines the fact that to establish MBO as a way of life in a company may take two or three years of sustained effort.

### WHY DO MANAGERS WITHHOLD SUPPORT?

However, even when the adviser understands his job and the board backs the program 100 percent, there will be problems if management down the line is not fully briefed on what management by objectives stands for in a total sense, as well as being briefed on the detailed mechanics.

On the face of it MBO looks incredibly simple. Many managers assume that they already know what is expected of them and that they already have effective standards and control procedures. *They are often cynical about a program which purports to help them to do these obvious things better.* So the briefing must be done personally, patiently, and imaginatively by senior management, as well as by the advisers. The way in which management by objectives integrates with existing systems in the business must be explained; otherwise it may appear to managers that an extra management system is being superimposed on one that already exists.

One major industrial concern, disappointed with the progress of its MBO program, wanted to find out why

17

many managers resisted the work in spite of top management's briefing and explicit support. An attitude survey showed fundamental reasons for this resistance:

- ☐ The business was highly profitable. Managers were not self-critical and said complacently, "Things are going well. Why change?"
- ☐ Good managers welcomed precise and challenging targets. Poor managers were justifiably insecure at the prospect of their inadequacy being revealed.
- ☐ Managers had no confidence that top management would persist with MBO. They had past experience of new techniques and methods being introduced and fading away unnoticed in a year or two.

Furthermore, managers who are asked to set their own objectives and therefore tell the truth about standards must be able to trust their superiors fully. When the briefing comes about, superiors must create a climate of confidence.

### QUANTIFYING EXPECTATIONS

An essential discipline of management by objectives is the attempt to quantify precisely what one is trying to achieve, individually and as a company. Generalized statements such as "We will increase our sales next year" give way to statements such as "We will increase our penetration of the French market by 4 percent by July 1974 with products A, B, and C."

Even in areas where at first sight it is difficult to find any standards at all, some progress can be made. For example, "Keep the company pension plan under review" can after analysis lead to the statement, "By the end of 1973 make a proposal to the managing director of the company for a pension program that will provide benefits which equal or exceed those offered in this area but with no increase in cost to employees or the company."

This insistence on quantification and measurable results is essential. However, a good MBO program also recognizes that there are *some* objectives which as yet, with our limited information, can be stated only in qualitative or subjective terms. This may not be desirable, but it is perhaps better to recognize areas which cannot be measured than to rely on inadequate measurable data. If one chooses the wrong quantitative standard, then dedicated effort may go in the wrong direction. Consider the example of the Veterans Administration given by Peter Drucker in *The Age of Discontinuity:*

> It may sound plausible to measure the effectiveness of a mental hospital by how well its beds—a scarce and expensive commodity—are utilized. Yet a study of the mental hospitals of the Veterans Administration brought out that this yardstick means mental patients being kept in the hospital—which, therapeutically, is about the worst thing that can be done to them. Clearly, however, lack of utilization, that is, empty beds, would also not be the right yardstick. How does one then measure whether a mental hospital is doing a good job within the wretched limits of our knowledge of mental diseases? [5]

Clearly, a company working in MBO has a delicate middle path to tread. On the one hand, it must insist on thinking through every key task and every important objective and spelling out as precisely and quantitatively as possible the result to be achieved. On the other, it must not allow people to concentrate on measured objectives to the exclusion of qualitative objectives, which may be even more important.

## LIMITATIONS OF STRATEGIC PLANNING

Many companies are stimulated by MBO to make their first strategic plan, and all the evidence shows that this is a fruitful piece of work. For example, the first attempt to plan long-term brings an integrating and unifying power to the group of managers at the top of the business. It is a catalyst of radical change rather than a minor improvement of the existing situation. It creates an attitude of mind focused more on tomorrow's opportunities than yesterday's mistakes. Certainly it facilitates communications up, down, and across the business, and compels serious thought about the correct sequence and methods of business planning from top to bottom in the organization.

However, strategic planning and its contribution can be overstated. It is not a substitute for an entrepreneur; it is not a magic and final answer, but rather a series of answers which are by a cascade approach constantly refined and improved. It certainly isn't easy work, and at some stages of company growth—for example, rapidly exploiting an unexpected opportunity— the full sequence may be inappropriate in its complete form for all companies.

A problem often raised by companies is, "Should objectives be changed if circumstances change during the planning period?" Obviously, this reflects a fear that to make a plan is to create inflexibility. In our experience, a well-based plan with the assumptions clearly stated and agreed upon is in fact a foundation for flexibility. When urgent decisions and changes have to be made, those involved start off with a common basis of knowledge and understanding and, therefore, perceptive and rapid change is facilitated. However, unless there are really significant changes in the premises on which the original plans were based, it is unwise to make too many changes. After all, the challenge for managers when the going gets rough is not to give up, but to find other means of reaching the agreed-upon goal.

### LINKING THE COMPANY'S OBJECTIVES
### TO THE INDIVIDUAL MANAGER'S RESULTS

Another problem to avoid is having each employee pursue his goal without taking into account the overall objectives of the company.

A French company, Photosia, found, for instance, that its sales and service departments, which had formerly worked closely together, were suffering from lack of communication.

What had happened was that after the introduction of MBO, the sales department had its set of objectives and no longer felt concerned about what occurred after the sale. Each one, they felt, should take care of his own objectives and not worry about his neighbor. To remedy the situation, management was obliged to set joint objectives shared by both departments.

The MBO system must ensure that individual managers' objectives mesh not only with their colleagues' objectives but also with total company goals.

An executive at Honeywell, Inc., interviewed by The Conference Board, said, "There are two things that might almost be considered fundamental creeds at Honeywell: decentralized management is needed to make Honeywell work, and management by objectives is needed to make decentralization work."

And to make MBO work there must be two elements: the *Key Results Analysis* and the *Job Improvement Plan*. Some companies believe that all that is required is to establish a series of personal objectives for achievement in a defined period. These selected areas are obviously chosen for their improvement potential, and managers are motivated to achieve these limited goals.

The problem arises when they achieve these goals by neglecting other important areas of the job. Success in the limited areas is defeated by losses elsewhere. However, if the manager is thoroughly instilled with the idea of the total success of the job, he loses grasp on *priorities*. Which area, he may ask himself, needs improvement? It is to handle this problem that the Job Improvement Plan concept exists.

The two work in tandem. The Key Results Analysis serves as the basis of achievement for the total job. It ensures that the manager *maintains* the important performance levels in line with company objectives. The Job Improvement Plan concentrates his attention on a limited number of tasks where results must *improve*. Increasingly, the Job Improvement Plan is the "brief" arising from a team or task force effort. The really substantial improvements can rarely be secured by the individual.

### REVIEW AND TRAINING

The review of the manager's performance and the review of his potential are two other touchy areas of MBO.

Problems revealed in an early British study are still common:

- Appraisers are reluctant to appraise.
- Interviewers are even more reluctant to interview.
- The follow-up is inadequate. Reports carry little or no weight when transfer, promotion, or training is considered.

If the MBO system is fully applied, the number of problems in this field should be reduced. Discussions usually improve because they are based substantially on agreed and, as far as possible, quantified goals. The man is encouraged to take the initiative with the boss as counselor rather than judge.

In addition, fewer ugly surprises should occur at review meetings. Review is not an isolated event once a year, but rather an additional occasion for taking a total view of results and resetting objectives. This total review supports an ongoing, day-to-day, week-to-week management review.

Potential review often creates problems because it is poorly handled. It is a subjective area, and common sense and discretion must be used in discussions with the manager. Very often some things should *not* be discussed at all. His superior should handle this delicate subject with advice from a staff expert such as the personnel manager if possible. Only thus can the manager's potential be put into context with the openings and career possibilities available throughout the firm.

Perhaps the word *needs* should be emphasized in this context. The organization needs an inventory of a man's performance and potential, in the most objective way possible, as a planning aid. Retirements are forecast, new subsidiaries will be opened, promotions have to be made—so the organization is looking at *its* needs to manage well its human resource. The manager's personal needs may be neglected . . . hence high labor turnover and frustration. All review procedures should include planned listening to the man's ambitions, the knowledge and experience he wants to acquire, the domestic problems which may temporarily inhibit mobility, and so on. The needs of the organization and those of the man must *both* be studied.

One further pitfall in the review field is to assume that all managers are endowed with the required level of personal skills in coaching and counseling. It's an assumption likely to lead to disappointment. We find it most constructive to give the managers planned learning experience in these coaching and counseling skills.

Training needs—from the company's, and again from the man's, viewpoint—are a spin-off from the MBO process. Yet many MBO systems are failing to produce perceptive needs analyses. There are still too many "package" courses and the indiscriminate use of outside courses. Why is this? Perhaps it's because managers are not aware of the facilities available. Do they sometimes blame the organization structure or poor planning, when further analysis shows it to be a gap in a man's knowledge and skills? Certainly, an MBO program which does not lead to economic and constructive plans for training is failing.

It is also easy to get sidetracked into concentrating on only *management* training.

In many cases, particularly at the middle and lower levels, success as a manager requires up-to-date technical knowledge. The over-concern with management training may lead to the neglect of identification of technical and administrative training needs.

The whole concept of management by objectives involves a deep consideration of control and information systems. They are required to provide focus of attention and feedback on the progress of key business and personal objectives. It is not surprising, however, that a number of companies run into problems with their control systems.

Usually this arises because they do not make a thorough analysis of the total control pattern. They improve separate pieces of information without looking at the relationship between the various parts. Even more dangerous is to focus attention—through control information—on unimportant matters.

An American cattle-feed manufacturing business did exactly this. It developed an extremely tight control over labor-staffing levels, utilization, and so on, while keeping its control information on material cost and yield primitive. Yet labor costs represented 12 percent of selling price and materials over 50 percent.

Another problem is that *additional controls are added without the company giving itself the discipline of removing a number of the existing ones.* Thus there is extra confusion and a proliferation of paper work. A management by objectives program should reduce the amount of existing control information while concentrating control patterns on the vital results areas.

G. J. Perkins suggested that it would be most helpful if MBO was invariably applied to the accounting function itself. For example, overall objectives might be:

□ To produce statutory returns which provide the shareholders and the public with a clear picture of

25

the significant financial data relating to the company and to make this information available at the earliest possible moment.

□ To provide management with all the information it requires in order to control the business efficiently, ensuring that such information is confined to truly significant data; that it is presented in a readily comprehensible manner; and is received by management within a time-scale which permits effective action to be taken to correct adverse trends.

□ To achieve these aims, including all supporting functions, at a minimum cost to the company.[6]

Against this framework, detailed action plans would be produced. Thus, as the MBO process motivates executive managers to identify clearly what control information they require, it can in parallel clarify and improve the service provided by accountants.

### SPECIAL PROBLEMS OF MBO IN THE NONPROFIT SECTOR

One of the most exciting developments in recent years has been the use of MBO by national and local government. Encouraging results have been secured in the Canadian Department of Fisheries and Forestry and in the Canadian Post Office.[7] In Britain 15 central government departments are using MBO, also major city governments, such as the Greater London Council.[8] It has become clear that MBO in the public sector requires new perceptions: business experience is not transferable without careful amendment to suit a different environment. As Peter Drucker has brought out with such clarity, the great distinguishing characteristic of the business institution is that it is an *economic* institution concerned *primarily* with economic performance and results: "This sets it apart from all other institutions of modern society, whether government, army, university, labor union, or hospital." These can and must be preoccupied with becoming more effective, but their raison d'être is fundamentally different.

It is not surprising that there are problems in "transferring" MBO knowledge—it is not easy to quantify results and to find common measures for comparing alternatives; the relationship between the politician and the permanent government officer is unlike the board of directors and senior executive relationship. Managers at all levels often rotate in their jobs to a degree unknown in business. In the end, the ultimate power for decision lies in the value judgments of the electorate. In a wider sense these issues are valid for the use of MBO in all nonprofit institutions, such as hospitals, the armed services, universities, and schools. Provided the fundamental concepts of MBO can be rethought to meet these special circumstances, the benefits can be significant. Indeed Sister Rosemary Miller, a member of the Presentation Sisters of the Blessed Virgin Mary, Aberdeen, South Dakota, has adapted the principles of MBO to a richer practice, "living by objectives." Challenging results are worked out in such key areas as community life, apostolates, personal development.[9]

### MAINTAINING MOMENTUM

Having ironed out all these problems, management may be tempted to sit back and take it easy. It will have forgotten another important aspect: *maintaining momentum*.

Certainly, there seems to be an extraordinary human capacity to convert the most exciting, vital, and dynamic concepts of management into dreary, mechanistic routines. Without imaginative plans to prevent this, MBO can deteriorate over a period of time.

As one president said of his experience of management by objectives: "Even where this concept of management has been completely built into the business and apparently accepted, it does need constant leadership to ensure that it is kept up to the mark."

One important way to maintain vitality is to keep the system under constant review. Paper work, for example, which was essential as an educational tool in the early stages of the program, might well be discarded once everybody has the habit of managing in this way.

### CONCLUSION

Management by objectives will create its own problems in the long run if it is not treated as an approach which must grow and develop organically to meet the changing needs of the business. This growth should not be haphazard. It must be planned and led by the top management team, and it must be given the same importance as developing new markets and new production facilities.

Avoiding the pitfalls of the MBO trap demands constant watching of the way the system is functioning. Is there proper communication from the lower levels of the company on up? Is the system being kept flexible? Are the objectives of both the company *and* its managers being kept flexible? Are the objectives of both the company and its managers being taken into account?

MBO is a two-sided system—one side technical, the other human. They are closely related, and putting the emphasis on one as opposed to the other is bound to lead to failure. Concentrating on performance goals or production levels and forgetting about the delegation of authority, the dialogue, and the individual's development and fulfillment is the surest way to fall headlong into the pit.

In Walter Wikstrom's words, "MBO does *not* succeed. However, men may succeed, using an MBO approach."

*Part Two*

---

# THE PRACTICE OF
# MANAGEMENT
# BY OBJECTIVES

## Essential Features and Benefits

Management by objectives is a dynamic system, which seeks to integrate a company's need to clarify and achieve its profit and growth goals with the manager's need to contribute and develop himself. It is a demanding and rewarding style of managing a business.

When a worthwhile system of management by objectives is operating in a company, there is a continuous process of:

- ☐ Reviewing critically and restating the company's *Strategic* and *Tactical Plans.*
- ☐ Clarifying with each manager the *Key Results* and *Performance Standards* he must achieve in line with unit and company objectives, and gaining his contribution and commitment to these individually and as a team member.
- ☐ Agreeing on a *Job Improvement Plan* with each manager, which makes a measurable and realistic contribution to the unit and company plans for better performance.
- ☐ Providing conditions in which it is possible to achieve the Key Results and carry out the Improvement Plan, notably an *organization structure* which gives a manager maximum freedom and flexibility

*Exhibit 3.*

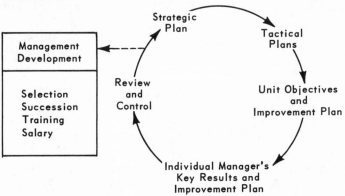

in operation, and *management control information* in a form and at a frequency which make for more effective self-control and better and quicker decisions.

□ Using systematic *Performance Review* to measure progress toward results and *Potential Review* to identify men with potential for advancement.

□ Developing *Management Training Plans* to help each manager to overcome his weaknesses, build on his strengths, and accept responsibility for self-development.

□ Strengthening a manager's motivation by effective *selection, salary,* and *succession plans.*

These techniques are interdependent. Exhibit 3 shows the dynamic nature of the system.

Two things follow: first, MBO is essentially the distillation into a workable system of the *best* practice already followed by managers. It is not something fashionable or new. As Exhibit 4 shows, MBO is a business process. Second, the development of managers, which

34

*Exhibit 4.*

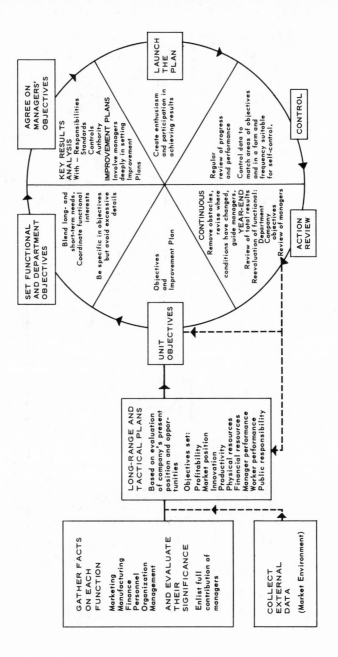

*Exhibit 5.*

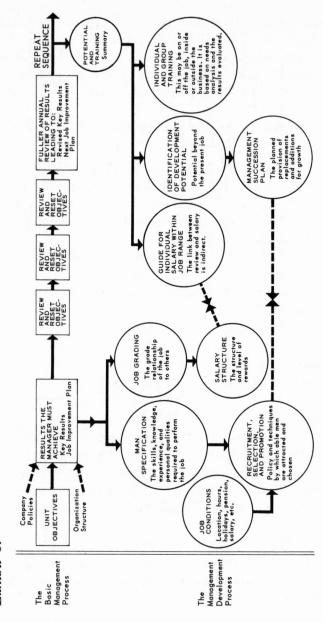

is a matter of vital importance to every company, makes sense only if it is integrated with the purpose of the business. Looked at in this way, management development is a valuable by-product of running a business efficiently. See Exhibit 5 for a schematic representation.

A successful management by objectives program furnishes these benefits to a company:

□ Concentration by people working on their own or as part of a team on the really important, profit-influencing tasks instead of dissipating energy on tasks which, even if done superbly well, could have little impact on overall results and growth.

□ A proper balance between innovation, flexibility, task-force work, and the need to work effectively in a well-designed hierarchy to keep the continuing business running well.

□ The identification of problems which prevent high performance, and improvement plans to solve them. In one engineering company, an analysis of the production manager's key results brought out weaknesses in process control which in turn led to a 12 percent reduction in scrap.

□ A demonstrable improvement in morale and sense of purpose arising from the involvement of managers. Labor turnover among key staff, which arose mainly from frustration, was reduced in a multiple retail concern within a year of introducing management by objectives.

□ The identification of men with potential so that reliable management succession plans can be built up. A large transport business found that its management succession plan was meaningless, since the technique of judging a manager's contribution to a business was defective and misleading.

□ Better management training at lower cost. A critical study of management training in a consumer durable manufacturing group showed that its content was mainly what the personnel department thought necessary and not the real needs, shown by performance review. A group of managers was being trained in report writing and communications when the urgent priority was for them to understand and use a new method of statistical quality control. People were sent to outside training courses with little consideration of individual special problems and with no provision for follow-up action on return.

□ Improvements in management controls and management performance standards. For example, it may be much more meaningful to express control data in tons per man-hour than in money, or to provide crude evidence of trends quickly rather than wait for more precise information. These points, to which lip service is often given, emerge vividly when controls are related to specific results which a manager agrees to achieve at a specific standard in a specific time.

□ Sounder organization structure with more effective delegation of responsibilities and accountability.

Typical benefits for an individual manager include:

□ Increased opportunity to make a personal contribution and to accept more responsibility.

□ Improved interpersonal relations through involvement in task forces to solve problems outside his own authority.

□ Less frustration as the framework of company ob-

38

jectives and the limits on his authority become clarified.

☐ Better, more purposeful communication about things that matter with his boss, colleagues, and subordinates.

☐ Increased opportunity for personal growth, strengthened by the knowledge that the company is systematically planning training and succession.

☐ Recognition of achievement by himself and his boss through clearer performance standards and sharper management controls.

☐ More equitable material rewards and promotion plans.

## What's Gone Wrong?

The management development programs which many progressive companies introduced after the Second World War claimed to provide many of the benefits we have listed. In fact, there is widespread recognition that most of these programs have not kept their promises. Robert J. House said bluntly:

> If enthusiasm and money could insure success, management development programs should be turning out managers enough for all industries. Yet the evidence is to the contrary. I have analyzed the results of 400 experimental studies concerned with management development and found much disappointment and disillusionment. In many cases, these programs have had little or no demonstrable or measurable effect on business performance or manager behavior.[1]

Those of us who introduced such programs with enthusiasm and sincerity should analyze frankly what's gone wrong. Without this evidence, the same mistakes may be repeated and the insistence on *depth* in our MBO work may seem exaggerated. The failures have been fundamental, not merely defects in techniques or procedures. The most common causes of failure are discussed in the following paragraphs.

### FAILURE TO INTEGRATE WITH THE COMPANY PROFIT PLAN

Every business requires objectives—short- and long-term, financial and nonfinancial—to be established after thorough study and evaluation of the present internal situation and the influence of outside environment. These objectives represent at any given time the best judgment of top management as to the course the business must take.

Consistent with these objectives, sub-objectives must be established for each division or subsidiary unit. The tragedy is that few managers really understand unit objectives and what their own contribution should be. Gray areas can lead to frustration as well-intentioned men strive for different and sometimes conflicting goals. It is a situation where managers are often judged by how busy they appear to be rather than by what relevant results they produce. In one company the production manager sought to increase throughput while maintaining quality. In fact, the forward sales position was poor and he should have been concentrating on how to keep unit costs low with reduced throughput; how to improve on delivery dates; how to improve quality. Management development has too often been a separate activity in the business, associated with the personnel department, and not seen as a dynamic means for executive management to link personal and company performance.

## STRESSING PERSONALITY RATHER THAN PERFORMANCE

When considering the appointment of a new works manager, the production director of a large engineering group was given staff appraisal forms of three superintendents. They were all highly rated in such terms as stability, adaptability, tact, and skill in decision making. He said, "These men look alright on paper but I'd rather have Smith," who was not included, "even if he rates only average. *Smith gets results.*" Too much effort has been put into the definition of an "ideal" manager's personality traits and not enough into judging how well he contributes to the company's success. To build an effective team we need a variety of personalities, not one stereotype endlessly repeated. A corollary of this preoccupation has been an undue emphasis on human relations training.

## PROGRAMITIS

Some companies have had too much faith in a mechanistic set of procedures, implicitly assuming that if people are appraised, sent on their quota of courses, and shown in a neat square on a replacement chart, all will be well. The problem has been made acute by extensive borrowing of other company procedures without any attempt to confirm that they are appropriate to the new situation. Good procedures are necessary, but they are subordinate to an analysis of a manager's work and the way in which his superior helps him improve. Douglas McGregor was right when he said that we need an agricultural analogy in "growing" talent rather than an industrial one of "manufacturing" it.[2]

At a deeper level, a manager has a great deal to contribute to the improvement of his job and the establishment of realistic objectives. Many management development programs have failed to secure this willing contribution. The manager must be personally involved at every stage and the whole approach should be flexible and human, not authoritarian and rigid.

### CROWN PRINCE COMPLEX

Radical changes in the educational structure make it essential to recruit young men at varying ages and levels of academic achievement. Each intake will require special plans. However, a common mistake is to believe management development problems are solved only by introducing a trainee scheme, especially when the scheme involves a year or two of watching without any weight of responsibility. Such a scheme must always be supported by a planned approach to improving performance for *all* managers on a *continuing* basis.

Too many systems have excluded the dark horses and poor starters. In a General Electric study, researchers dug out a list of 143 "promising young men" of ten years ago and followed up on their careers. Only 37 percent had achieved the success predicted for them at the time of appraisal.[3]

### OVEREMPHASIS ON PROMOTION

Most management development programs overemphasize promotion. This influences managers to devote too much to the future instead of concentrating on achieving first-class results on their present job. They become frustrated because advancement never seems to come as quickly as expected. Promotion is important and a manager should be helped to enlarge his capacity and experience for a bigger job. But he should earn advancement mainly by outgrowing the present job. Promotion should be a ladder, requiring effort and sacrifice to climb, not an escalator. Development is primarily a manager's own responsibility, although the company must provide stimulus and opportunity.

### ABDICATION BY EXECUTIVE MANAGEMENT

Specialist personnel departments have often taken staff development responsibility from managers, implying that it is too complex and specialized for laymen. Line managers have often been glad to relinquish this responsibility. If the view of management development as a work-centered activity is accepted, it follows that every manager is responsible for setting objectives for his staff, training them, judging their performance, and encouraging them. It is a responsibility that cannot be delegated. Personnel specialists should be advisers and counselors in this to line managers.

### PURSUIT OF FASHIONABLE TECHNIQUES

Some companies seem to have no stability in developing their managers. They pursue each fashionable technique or idea with enthusiasm, seeing it as the panacea for all ailments.

*43*

"It's important to communicate with foremen.

Let's have a newsletter and a conference every three months."

"There's a new course on decision making.

We must send all our managers to it."

"Sensitivity training is the breakthrough we need.

After all, we have to work in groups to get things done."

The technique may have genuine merit, but it must be seen in perspective as just one part of a continuous and developing interrelationship between objectives, personal results, review, training, and wider opportunity.

### MANAGEMENT DEVELOPMENT AS AN ACT OF FAITH

Large sums of money have been invested by companies on in-plant management development activities. It is usually accepted that a measurable return cannot be expected from this money. "After all, education must always be an act of faith," said one personnel director.

It is true that some aspects of manager development are intangible. It is equally true that the really effective development plans are regarded as economic activities of the business. When their costs are challenged, they can be justified often in positive, identifiable improvements in jobs and managers. Where this wish to evaluate critically is absent, management development becomes a flabby complacent routine.

## Three Points of View

By now we know with complete confidence that management development cannot *alone* solve the problems which concern MBO. It is a vitally important *part* of MBO, but a wider viewpoint is necessary. Let us look at the problem of developing managers in line with company objectives from the viewpoint of the chief executive, of one of his managers, and of the management team.

### THE CHIEF EXECUTIVE

In the last 15 years or so there has been a phenomenal increase in the United States in the use of comprehensive business planning on a corporate basis. Professor George A. Steiner estimates that at least 75 percent of the largest industrial companies are so organized. He attributes this growth to such factors as a stronger belief that, far from being helpless in the face of market forces, a business can increasingly determine where it will go in the future. Moreover, the sheer complexity of the management task and the rate of environmental change compel a more systematic approach.[4] It is hardly surprising that chief executives concentrate more time on planning. A recent study of 280 chief executives showed that 65 percent of them identified their most important activity as long-range planning. They said they spend 44 percent of their time on it.[5]

Urwick, Orr & Partners Ltd. made a study [6] of the attitude of chief executives toward the problem of developing their managers. It appears that the rapid growth of interest in recent years is due to six main pressures.

First, the *increased complexity of a manager's job* in the face of an accelerating rate of technological change, the larger size of business, and the introduction of new techniques such as operational research caused concern. Many managers are inadequate because the job has outgrown them. "Management obsolescence" is a genuine issue, not a conference joke. It is recognized that unless much more attention is given at the planning stage to developing people's knowledge and skills, important projects and techniques will be stultified.

Second, the *failure to produce enough men of general management outlook*. The shortage of general managers has been particularly evident in the large companies which have decentralized their operations and have had to face complex new problems of coordination and control. The need to ensure that specialists improve their performance and that there is an opportunity to move into wider responsibilities is accepted.

Overspecialization for too long has become common, however, and chief executives believe that there is now no alternative to selecting a group of able men, relatively young, and grooming them deliberately for general management.

Third, *succession problems* are commonplace in every type of business. Some chief executives admitted that they were now interested in management development because they had lost key executives and found no one remotely eligible to replace them from within the business. The ratio of managers to workforce is much higher than it used to be and calls for a greater number of managers. Since the problem is universal, the main solution is recognized as "developing our own men" rather than constantly trying to buy talent.

Fourth, there are *doubts whether the money invested so far in management development, company training centers, and so on has been really well spent.* "I'm sure we have done something. I'm equally sure our past efforts have not been wholly successful. But I'm continuing them as an insurance policy until something better emerges," was one comment. This is in striking contrast to the enthusiasm and confidence of the small number of chief executives who have introduced a management by objectives approach and discovered the lasting benefits.

Fifth, there was frank admission that *companies had grown complacent in an easy sellers' market.* Managers brought up in this easygoing atmosphere were concerned with security, not risk taking and innovation. "One reason why I've decentralized my operating units is to put back into people a sense of responsibility for profit and loss. How else will we create vitality and growth?" said the managing director of one engineering group.

There is also the problem of what to do with a manager who, after many chances, cannot or will not match up to the job standard. "Let's face it, most of us lack the moral courage to deal with this as we should, especially when it is a man who has given his life to the business," was one view. Probably it represents a general truth, even though other chief executives were quick to point out that firmness in these cases was in the interests not only of the business but also of the man himself.

Another view was: "My philosophy is to set a time limit and a measurable target for minimum performance and then pull the stops out to help the man succeed. If he doesn't, I instantly remove him from his post although I then treat him with generous and humane consideration."

Sixth, those companies with overseas subsidiaries usually commented on the *pressures of nationalism.* Long-term plans to hand over to nationals were having to be compressed into much shorter periods. It was felt that more attention would have to be given to analyzing the present managerial knowledge and skills in detail, thus making it possible for more concentrated instruction to be given.

Compared with a similar study made some years ago, there was a widespread and fundamental change in attitude. Chief executives today recognize more than ever before that their managers are a precious capital resource which requires the same systematic attention as financial and physical resources.

Asked what they wanted from a management development program, chief executives said:

- To have an effective method of defining results expected from managers.
- To get managers continuously to improve their performance.
- To secure and hold recruits of suitable caliber.
- To provide first-class training, for tomorrow's job as well as today's, at lower cost.
- To have a reliable means of judging the performance of managers.
- To have a flexible succession plan for staffing the business in the future.
- To motivate managers and reward them fairly in relation to the results achieved.
- To improve the flow of communications up, down, and across the business.

It is illuminating to see these views in relation to the manager's needs. A typical manager, when asked "What do you want from me, your boss, in order to perform your job better?" would state five needs:

| The Manager's Needs | Methods Available to Help the Manager |
|---|---|
| Be sure we agree on what you expect from me | Clarifying *Unit Objectives* and priorities for improvement<br>*Key Results Analysis* with performance standards<br>*Job Improvement Plans* |
| Give me an opportunity to perform | *Organization Planning* |
| Let me know how I'm getting on | *Control Information*<br>*Performance Review* |
| Give me guidance where I need it | *Management Development Methods*<br>—Potential review<br>—Training |
| Reward me according to my contribution | —Salary structure<br>—Succession plans |

This simple analysis stresses the *interrelationship* of needs, and therefore of supporting methods and techniques. To train a manager without a clear grasp of the skills and knowledge required to secure results can be frustrating. The influence of a good salary structure on motivation can be slight if the manager is bewildered about the nature of his responsibilities. Control information devised by staff specialists alone may prove to be irrelevant to the manager's needs.

Thus, success must come from the continuous satisfaction of *all* the manager's needs and not from spasmodically improving isolated techniques.

### THE MANAGEMENT TEAM

Individual accountability for results, self-control and self-direction, a concern with the unique training and development needs of a man—these are all vital features of management by objectives.

Overstated, however, individualism can lead to selfishness and a narrow view of responsibility which injures the total company's interests. In any case, neither the chief executive nor his manager can succeed in isolation, since they are both dependent on team support and cooperation of colleagues. Management teams and groups are becoming ever more important for success as business becomes more complex in structure, technology, size, and human relationships.

The problem in practice is one of balance, since both individual and group methods have an appropriate contribution to make. Much of the confusion in discussion about this subject is stirred up by extreme views, ranging from: "A camel is a horse put together by a committee," to "No decision should be made unless it has been discussed and willingly approved by all the management team."

Perhaps it is understandable that the importance of teamwork has not been properly recognized. Most of us have had the frustrating experience of being a member of a committee or group where the purpose of the meeting was unclear, where a few people dominated the discussion, or where several people present were there solely to protect the marginal interests of their department. Most of us can remember meetings in which people didn't really listen, or where lively disagreement and differences were quickly smothered.

However, this situation only justifies an attack on *bad* teamwork, not teamwork itself. In a brilliant paper,[7] the late Douglas McGregor suggested the unique features of an effective managerial team. They can be summarized as:

1. *Understanding, mutual agreement, and identification with respect to the primary task*

2. *Open communications*

    If the ideas, facts, and arguments are not put on the table, the group cannot take them into account.

3. *Mutual trust*

    McGregor defines trust this way: "I know that you will not—deliberately or accidentally, consciously or unconsciously—take unfair advantage of me." As he points out, "Trust is a delicate property of human relationships. It is influenced far more by actions than by words. It takes a long time to build, but it can be destroyed very quickly."

4. *Mutual support*

5. *Management of human differences*

    Differences are a major asset, since from them come all innovation, all creative problem solutions. But certain differences can destroy an organization. Without some norms and rules anarchy can result. Successful management of differences is an essential characteristic of an effective management team.

6. *Selective use of the team*
   Use the team for *team* activities and delegate to individuals or subgroups other activities.

7. *Appropriate member skills*
   These team skills are different from those of a work team performing, for example, a mining task. They include, among others, seeking information, giving information, summarizing.

8. *Leadership*
   The personal qualifications and skills and the role and strategy of the manager of the team should not be undervalued, but some of the necessary characteristics of the effective team cannot be determined by the leader alone.

It is interesting that McGregor includes in his list the *selective* use of the team and advises us to keep the team concept in perspective. One factor to consider is the high cost of management time and money when a group is trying to do a job better done by an individual! Moreover, the marvelous personal leadership of some individuals and the instinctive approach of the true entrepreneur would be ignored at our peril.

The MBO practice does, of course, involve teamwork in various ways. For example:

☐ The top management group will work together to analyze strengths and weaknesses, threats and opportunities, and so commit itself to a forward strategy.

☐ A manager will not *only* work with his individual subordinates in clarifying their objectives, he will bring the subordinates together to work as a team on common problems, horizontal cross-linking of standards and controls, and ideas for improvement.

☐ Complex and significant *business* problems can rarely be solved by work within one function. A normal part of MBO is to set up *Task Forces* which are not bound by functional structure. They explore opportunities and threats within a company key area. Basically, the form of a matrix analysis for a medium-size manufacturing company is as shown in Exhibit 6.

Thus a Task Force to study a company strategy for industrial relations would probably include the general manager, plant manager, and personnel manager. However, since it is knowledge, not status, that is the criterion for membership, there may be a subordinate, say, of the plant manager who should be a Task Force member.

The future complexity of business will compel managers to fulfill two roles. As a manager responsible for, say, production or sales, his main commitment with his colleagues is to achieve the agreed-upon objectives with maximum effectiveness. There will be some areas entirely within their control where they can secure im-

*Exhibit 6.*

| Key Area \ Position | General Manager | Marketing Manager | Plant Manager | Personnel Manager | Accountant |
|---|---|---|---|---|---|
| Industrial Relations | √ | X | √ | √ | X |

√ — major influence on success or failure
X — little influence on success or failure

provement. The same manager may from time to time be a working member of a Task Force, set up to clarify and make recommendations for change and improvement in a vital area of the business. Invariably such areas do not fit into the conventional executive structure. "Shall we open an operation in Europe?" calls for contributions from marketing, finance, production, and other authorities. In such a Task Force it is the authority of knowledge which matters, not formal status. Undoubtedly it is in these multilevel, multidiscipline Task Forces where major innovative thought can be generated. If it is to happen constructively, the Task Force must set itself clear objectives and learn to work together well. A far cry from committees on the one hand and free-form organization on the other! [8]

So far we have considered the team question in the context of the type of organization where the dominant way in which the ongoing business is managed is through individuals and groups of managers in the functional departments. The Task Force is the temporary "innovative" or problem-solving instrument. However, there are many situations where the need is different; in construction projects and research and development work, for example, the dominant way to manage the ongoing business is by a *project* approach. R. J. Wills of Urwick Technology Management points out [9] that the essence of a project is its transient nature; the quality of decisions made must be of a very high order because it is a once-only activity. The contributors to the project will often be a *unique team*—the people have to work together quickly and effectively in a situation where new problems are inevitable since no projects are ever quite alike. The features of a well-managed project, which are listed in Exhibit 7, clearly suggest that the knowledge and interpersonal skills of a project team must be of the highest order.

With all these different team situations inherent in the MBO process, one further problem emerges: how to help them to be more effective as a work group. In one widely used practical approach to group training, a skilled observer is present with a real group trying to solve a real problem: his contribution is that of analyst and coach.

First, the group has to think through its goals. Just what is it trying to achieve? This must be made explicit and agreed upon with the participation and commitment of group members. Until this is done well, the best way each member can help is not clear.

Second, an adaptation of Bales's Interaction Process Analysis [10] enables the observer to see how individuals are reacting within the group. Twelve categories, such as "Gives suggestions," "Gives opinion," "Gives orientation," "Disagrees," and so on, are noted, typically in 15-minute samples. The development of computer programs for on-line processing enables rapid processing of observations, so that the group quickly gets feedback on such matters as the extent to which the group is structuring the problem rather than assuming its nature, and the extent to which members are being frank and open. Participants are also able to get some insights about the individual members and their dominant styles. They can discuss their performance as a group.

Certainly this approach to team training has proved a practical, simple, and highly effective way to improve group productivity. This happens as they learn

**Exhibit 7.** Features of a well-managed project.

A well-managed project is one in which:

- The purpose (what is wanted as the end result, and why, and the chance of failure which is acceptable) is known, and accords with company policy as it reflects company needs.
- Factors are identified which would place constraints on implementation of a successful result from the project.
- The *real* problem, taking account of constraints, is identified.
- Key stage-by-stage objectives are established (if necessary as the result of a series of iterations, each involving the accumulation of more information).
- Objective-setting includes the identification of:
  1. Existing technical and commercial information.
  2. Applications of the end result of the project, particularly those which capitalize on its properties.
  3. User requirements, for functional properties and for economics of application.
  4. Application constraints, imposed by user.
  5. Market assessments when applicable (volume, price, competitive situation).
- Criteria are established for knowing whether the chosen objectives have been reached.
- The broad range of alternative ways of solving the problem is assessed before effort is concentrated in particular directions.
- Acceptable limits are established for the calendar time and the expenditure to the conclusion of each stage.
- Project stages are defined.
- The resource needs are identified (people, skills, knowledge, facilities, materials, and cash).
- Plans are made to match resource availability to needs.
- The tasks necessitated by the project, whether for its planning or its execution, are carried out in an economical and timely manner, without duplication of effort or gaps in the program.
- Feedback of information is used to change resources and targets as necessary and implementation action ensues.

*Prepared by R.J. Wills and P. Kendrick*

together to follow a sequential problem-solving approach and monitor their achievements.

In this field we should let McGregor have the last word:

> Perhaps it is now clear why an effective management team seldom just happens. It is a complex and delicate system, the building and maintenance of which requires much time and attention. Its contribution to the achievements of the goals of the enterprise can, however, be well worth the effort devoted to its creation.[11]

## Making a Start

There is no one right way to launch a program of management by objectives. However, experience suggests that the following points are especially important.

☐ Secure the support, understanding, and positive commitment of the chief executive and his senior colleagues. It is impossible for a simple man-to-man target-setting type of exercise, initiated, say, by a personnel department in isolation, to make a lasting impact on company performance. MBO must be seen as a serious and complex project if it is to get to the heart of problems and change behavior. It follows that support from the top is a prerequisite for success.

☐ Make a careful study of the business to determine the best starting point. Is a pilot piece of work necessary? Or will a wide-scale attack serve the company better, even though quality will inevitably be uneven?

What is the present method of defining and achieving objectives? What is the present organization structure—is it so inappropriate that adjustment is necessary before MBO in any disciplined sense is practicable? What is the existing management information pattern? What are the relationships between people—their motivation and commitment? Is there an existing management development program and, if so, what are its strengths and weaknesses?

☐ Select and train one or more advisers who will help to launch the work. These should be men of high caliber assigned to this work temporarily. After thorough training they can fill an invaluable role as catalysts and advisers on the best techniques and methods. In small companies the adviser will be part time and may be the chief executive himself.

☐ Brief all managers thoroughly so that the purpose, benefits, and stages of the program are fully understood.

☐ Critically examine the total company objectives before, or at least in parallel with, the analysis of individual jobs. Use Task Forces to get to the heart of complex, significant threats and opportunities in key business areas.

☐ Work in complete units, or subunits, from top to bottom so that *all* managers are included. It is a mistake to attempt to improve the performance of a horizontal level. (For example: "We'll introduce the program for our foremen but not for senior management.")

☐ Start in the main profit-influencing part of the business, typically sales and production, and then move on to the supporting service and staff departments such as personnel and accounts.

☐ Working simultaneously from the top of the business down and from the lowest level of management up, it is possible to collect rich data on improvement possibilities. This can lead to first coordinated *Unit* and *Job Improvement Plans*.

□ Avoid rushing the program merely to produce a collection of forms quickly. Patience, thoroughness, and perseverance are essential if new behavior is to be created and the *real* problems exposed. Although short-term gains are quickly evident, a full launching will generally take about a year to get the full first cycle of work going in a unit. It will take another year or two of top management follow-through to *consolidate* the program as a way of life.

Exhibit 8 shows a typical launching sequence, but it must be emphasized that each situation will require separate analysis and its own launching sequence.

### THE ROLE OF THE ADVISER

When introducing MBO into a company, it is necessary to use one or more company advisers. This is an essential but temporary job with three responsibilities:

1. *As a change agent*

   The adviser can make a great contribution in human terms, sitting in as a catalyst at man/boss discussions; helping task forces and teams to work effectively; briefing people; observing strains and tensions inevitable in a period of change and renewal; and helping the people concerned to solve the problems.

2. *As a teacher or counselor*

   After 15 years or so there is a great deal of know-how about MBO. It would be absurdly wasteful if each company and each manager started on MBO

*Exhibit 8.* Typical launching sequence.

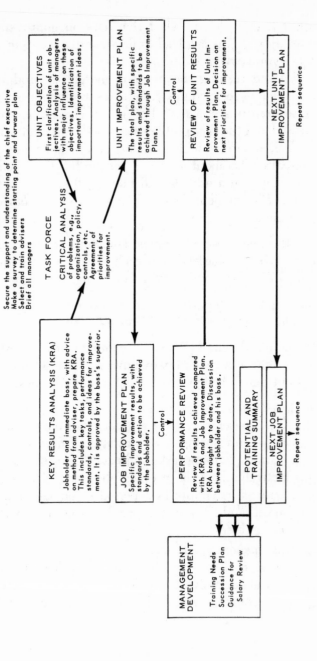

PRELIMINARY WORK

Secure the support and understanding of the chief executive
Make a survey to determine starting point and forward plan
Select and train advisers
Brief all managers

TASK FORCE

CRITICAL ANALYSIS
of problems, e.g., organization, policy, controls, etc. Agreement of priorities for improvement.

UNIT OBJECTIVES

First clarification of unit objectives. Analysis of managers with major influence on these objectives. Identification of important improvement ideas.

UNIT IMPROVEMENT PLAN

The total plan, with specific results and standards to be achieved through Job Improvement Plans.

REVIEW OF UNIT RESULTS

Review of results of Unit Improvement Plan. Decision on next priorities for improvement.

Control

NEXT UNIT IMPROVEMENT PLAN

Repeat sequence

KEY RESULTS ANALYSIS (KRA)

Jobholder and immediate boss, with advice on method from adviser, prepare KRA. This includes key tasks, performance standards, controls, and ideas for improvement. It is approved by the boss's superior.

JOB IMPROVEMENT PLAN

Specific improvement results, with standards and action to be achieved by the jobholder.

Control

PERFORMANCE REVIEW

Review of results achieved compared with KRA and Job Improvement Plan. KRA brought up to date. Discussion between jobholder and his boss.

POTENTIAL AND TRAINING SUMMARY

NEXT JOB IMPROVEMENT PLAN

Repeat sequence

MANAGEMENT DEVELOPMENT

Training Needs
Succession Plan
Guidance for Salary Review

without access to this accumulated knowledge and practical experience. The adviser can give personal coaching and can contribute to briefing and training sessions on all aspects of MBO. He should be a learning resource for the company in the launching stage.

3. *As an administrator*

Inevitably there is some administration. Someone has to make the appointments, plan the overall program, and so on. It may be pedestrian work and is certainly the least important part of the adviser's job, but it must be done and done well if the launching is to go smoothly.

The adviser is invariably an in-company man of the right quality and acceptability, seconded to help with the MBO launch partly as a feature of his own personal development plan.

### THE ROLE OF THE OUTSIDE CONSULTANT

The outside consultant acts as the adviser at the highest level—for example, in the discussions between the chief executive and his immediate subordinates and in contributing to the thinking on purpose, key areas, and company objectives. Quite apart from the breadth of different experience the consultant can bring to bear, it is virtually impossible politically for an in-company adviser to operate at this level.

The outside consultant also trains the in-company advisers in the most up-to-date practice of MBO. This will be done in courses on the job and then by supervision and guidance in the early phases of the adviser's work.

No matter how competent the adviser or sincere the managers, the successful introduction of Key Results, Improvement Plans, and Performance Reviews depends on the senior executive of the company or operational unit concerned. One president, introducing MBO, said to his subordinates, "We are going to start by sorting out together what we are trying to achieve, how we can measure and control this, and how we can do a better job. Let's have the truth and be honestly prepared to lift the stones and see what is underneath, even if it crawls onto our desk. Above all, let no one recriminate about past failures, but rather let us concern ourselves with tomorrow and a better result."

This epitomizes the right attitude of mind for lasting success.

## Setting Objectives

As the typical launching sequence indicates, the starting point must invariably be the first clarification of company (or operating unit) objectives. When the early work on this does not expose any major changes— for example, a fundamentally different type of organization pattern—it is then desirable to analyze the departmental and individual manager results in parallel with the continuing work on company objectives. Thus at a certain time the wishes of the top management team can be refined and challenged by practical experience and ideas from lower management levels. Once a final decision is made, Improvement Plans can be issued with the confidence that all managers have shared in creating them and are motivated to get results.

At the company level, the analytical process will usually include the top team grappling with *purpose*, asking such fundamental questions as:

What business are we really in?
What are the specific needs of our customers?
Which markets are we trying to meet?

This may sound like a rather academic starting point, but it isn't! Nothing is more salutary than to have half a dozen top managers write down individually their definition of the basic company purpose, its raison d'être, and then to look together at all these definitions.

The next step is to determine the *Key Areas*—those groups of management activities which need to be coordinated to produce an important result. Drucker's list is:

Business(es)
Profitability
Innovation
Market standing
Productivity
Financial and physical resources
Manager performance and development
Worker performance and attitude
Public responsibility

There is nothing sacred about this list—it should be used as a starter to thinking about the Key Areas which suit each company.

It is then necessary to *search for improvement* through a critical analysis of strengths and weaknesses, threats and opportunities, in each or a limited number of particularly important Key Areas. This search is invariably done best by Task Forces, rather than individual managers.

Now *policies,* or the accepted "decision rules" with which the company is at present living, may also be critically examined to ensure that they are up to date and relevant.

*Control and information* systems must be examined.

Finally, on the basis of stated *assumptions,* it is possible to set out explicitly the *company objectives.*

This approach is flexible, of course, and varies according to the degree of sophistication of existing company planning, the urgency of problems faced, and so on. It is essential, however, to have a disciplined approach which directly involves the top management team. The members must feel completely committed to the final decisions taken.

In larger companies, the support of long-range or corporate planning staff is often of great importance. Recognizing the complexity of the process, companies such as IBM, Xerox, W. R. Grace, and General Electric have found it helpful to divide the corporate planning staff into two groups—strategic planning and operational planning.

It may help to consider the basic thinking which underlies this disciplined approach to setting objectives.

The central objective of a company must be to maximize the long-term return on resources which it employs. Planning for profit must be done in the context of a critical analysis of the company's strengths and weaknesses, of the threats and opportunities arising from the external environment in which it operates, and of the expectations of the owners, employers, employees, and customers. A critical analysis of this kind, projected several years ahead, invariably demonstrates action to secure immediate improvements. More important, it leads to the development of long-term strategic plans which deal with such things as future markets, the planned return on investment from individual markets and products, the elimination of non-profit-making activities, and diversification. In my view, the real value of making the first Strategic Plan is educational. It gives discipline to the collection of important facts and—more important—stimulates top management as a team to interpret the data and ask these fundamental questions:

- What *is* our real business?
- What rate of return on assets are we determined to achieve?
- Are we going to achieve this merely by making our present business more efficient? Or should we not think of bolder moves such as divestment of low-growth products and divisions and acquisition of high-growth companies that will fit the pattern of the business we are trying to create?
- Is the quality, motivation, and knowledge of our management team adequate to meet future demands which will be made on them?
- Are we allowing high-quality resources to drift into low-opportunity areas?

This may seem a tedious way to reach the same conclusion that an outstanding entrepreneur will have reached quickly on the basis of experience, flair, and intuition. It is. Unfortunately, entrepreneurs of this caliber seem to be in rather short supply.

Once the Strategic Plan is established, supporting Tactical Plans can be worked out in such areas as organization changes, product/market development, al-

65

location of financial and physical resources, operational tasks. In turn, these, through Key Results Analysis, can become the responsibility of individual managers. This hierarchy of objectives is illustrated in Exhibit 9.

Of course, every company and unit has objectives, even where they are not explicitly stated, particularly in such areas as production, sales, and finance. Frequently these objectives are narrowly conceived and too short in time span; for example, to overconcentrate on one objective, such as return on capital, can lead to a distortion of management effort no matter how important that objective may be. To stress this year's profit target as the sole criterion for management success will inhibit developments which are vital for long-term growth.

To illustrate the questions to be considered in the detailed analysis, we can look at six examples of Key Areas:

> Finance and profitability
> Market position
> Product innovation and development
> Staff development
> Productivity and physical resources
> Organization

### FINANCE AND PROFITABILITY

This central expression of corporate objectives should be identified over the individual phases of the planning period and should include:

1. *Turnover*
   To be expressed in values and in physical units under the various product headings.

*Exhibit 9.* Simplified MBO chart; typical hierarchy of objectives.

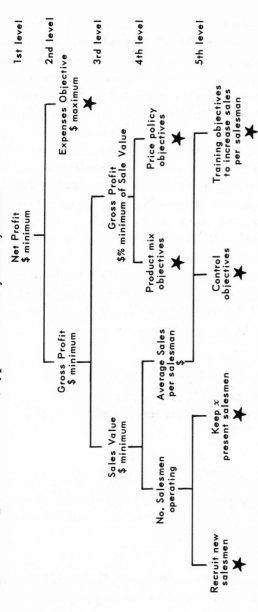

Note 1
This example is not complete: there are likely to be many more objectives at each level. The symbol ★ indicates that no contributive objectives have been specified.

Note 2
All the objectives shown are abbreviated. To be useful, they must be specified clearly enough to ensure that all concerned understand the same thing.

## 2. Gross margins

To be shown under key product groupings.

## 3. Overheads

Statement to include the major contributions to fixed charges and to be related to the varying pattern of activity planned.

## 4. Net profit and return on investment

It is characteristic of a complex business that it may be necessary to employ more than one of the main expressions of return on investment for different sections of the plan. These may include return on gross assets, or net assets, or total assets, and on shareholders' equity.

## 5. Derived objectives

The establishment of the main profit objectives will determine other derived objectives under this heading which must be reconciled both with the main profit objectives and with one another. These will include:

(a) Rate of stock turn.

(b) Investment in working capital.

(c) Short- and long-term financial resources.

(d) The range of operating ratios.

### MARKET POSITION

The most important objectives to be set include:

## 1. Total market volume

Expressed in terms of:

(a) Coverage

(b) Penetration

Is it growing at a pace which offers sufficient scope for a greater market share at an acceptable cost?

2. *Prospective buyers*
   Identification of key accounts to be developed. Are
   we directing our resources to those buyers who will
   produce the turnover, profit, and growth needed?
3. *Locating numbers and types of existing buyers*
   The accessibility of the buyer and his likely special
   requirements must be forecast if the organization
   is to determine which market objectives are to have
   priority.

### PRODUCT INNOVATION AND DEVELOPMENT

1. *Short-term developments*
   In the early stages of the plan it is often impractic-
   able to make a significant extension of range. The
   most important immediate steps may well be to
   agree on objectives for:
   (a) The removal of unprofitable products.
   (b) The redirection of resources to secure im-
       provements in existing products and a heavier
       concentration on their market development.
2. *Long-term developments*
   To cover the program of longer-term additions to
   the product range and to be related to the research
   resources available. It is characteristic of this aspect
   of planning that the objectives should indicate
   whether the particular product extensions will
   come from:
   (a) Own technical development.
   (b) Licensing arrangements.
   (c) Cooperative marketing or merger.
3. *Market changes*
   Objectives relating to the changes sought in market
   pattern including:

(a) Division as between home and export markets.
(b) Individual geographical markets.
(c) Particular consuming sectors of the market. Thus in the case of capital goods this may include sales to be made to a particular industry (for example, motor industry, textiles) or in the case of consumer goods the target sales for particular socioeconomic or age groups.

It is important that the objectives set under these headings be reconciled with the resources available for both technical development and market promotion.

## STAFF DEVELOPMENT

The objectives set under the first three key areas above will require a reappraisal of the staff resources necessary to achieve them throughout the period of the plan. These will cover both managers and labor force and will include such objectives as:

- The preparation of management succession plans.
- Recruitment objectives for specified types of managerial and technical skills.
- Training plans.
- The introduction of specific forms of motivation (including forms of incentive and wage payments).
- The setting of limits to labor and staff turnover.

## PRODUCTIVITY AND PHYSICAL RESOURCES

Objectives under this heading will be related to the commercial objectives set out under the first two Key Areas and will include specific aims under the headings of:

1. *Volume targets for output*
   Under product groups and individual plants.

2. *Cost objectives*
   To cover key items such as labor, materials, scrap rates, labor costs, overhead.

3. *Plant and equipment*
   Objectives to cover location of new plants and introduction of new component and manufacturing processes to meet sales objectives over the planning period.

4. *Distribution facilities*
   The objectives in the establishment of warehousing and depot facilities and corresponding transport plans.

5. *Labor requirements*
   To establish a phased program of objectives to cover numbers and types of labor necessary to meet the commercial objectives.

The time span of objectives under this group tends to be longer than certain of the commercial objectives to which they relate and some reconciliation is necessary at each stage of the planning process.

### ORGANIZATION

Objectives in developing the organization should reflect the objectives set under the previous headings and will include the need to identify the following aims:

1. *Basis of company or legal entity*
   Are any changes in the legal structure of the company necessary to meet the objectives effectively? These will include changes in location, problems of

minority interests, the change of status from private to public form, and so on.

2. *Realignment of functions*

Objectives under this heading will include measures of centralization or delegation of authority and in some cases will even specify the introduction of a totally new function to the company (for example, research and development or operational research department).

3. *Reappraisal of lines of authority*

Existing structure may show that the responsibility for achieving objectives is not matched by the authority of executives concerned or by their supporting services. The revision of the scope of the authority of these executives should be planned as part of the pattern of objectives.

4. *Subdivision of tasks*

The examination of objectives may show that there is a concentration of responsibility for their achievement which:

(a) Exceeds the acceptable limits of an individual job.

(b) Makes for undue vulnerability.

Objectives should be set for planning a division of responsibility for achievement in these cases.

A common error in establishing objectives is to plan for too rapid a rate of change in organization structure. It is necessary that such objectives should be phased to meet only the essential requirements of the basic objectives of the business.

Charles H. Granger points out how even a small amount of clarification can greatly increase the effectiveness of a business and suggests some minimum tests which objectives should meet. He says that objectives

> . . . need not begin with the broad grand design of the enterprise, but all objectives in the hierarchy should be consistent with it.
> . . . should make the people in the enterprise reach a bit.
> . . . should be realistic in terms of (a) the internal resources of the enterprise and (b) the external opportunities, threats, and constraints.
> . . . should take into account the creative conception of a range of alternatives and the relative effectiveness and cost of each.
> . . . should be known to each person so that he understands the goals of his own work and how they relate to the broader objectives of the total enterprise.
> . . . should be periodically reconsidered and redefined, not only to take account of changing conditions, but for the salutary effect of rethinking the aims of organization activities.[12]

Setting objectives of this kind is a searching discipline with three important implications:

First, those companies which do not *plan* to create and capitalize on growth opportunities are unlikely to profitably survive the pressures of competition in the long term (although it must be admitted that some companies appear to have a remarkable built-in capacity to survive in spite of persistent bad management).

Second, to go no further than clarifying divisional or sectional goals encourages a partisan and selfish attitude: "As long as I get my results I'm in the clear, whatever the overall situation." When managers can see their unit's contribution integrated with the *total* organization goals, cooperation is encouraged.

Third, without the challenge and sense of purpose provided by demanding company objectives, management development has no real meaning. Where the two are blended together, the impact can be remarkable and we begin to see, in Robert H. Schaffer's words:

> . . . the power of imaginative, clear-cut, and inspiring goals to evoke extraordinary performance from people—*and* the power of these goals to help groups merge efforts and produce joint results which transcend the simple sum of their individual capacities.[13]

Exhibits 10 to 14 show the thinking underlying the setting of objectives at corporate level and integrating them with individual objectives at AB Svenska Kullagerfabriken (SKF), the Swedish ball bearing company, which has a majority interest in almost 130 firms around the world with sales over $900 million. In recent years SKF has developed an integrated approach to long-range planning, MBO, information systems, and management development.

*Exhibit 10.*

---

**THE FOUR KEY ISSUES OF CORPORATE PLANNING IN THE SKF GROUP**

* Long-range planning based on predetermined, agreed objectives requires and stimulates opportunity seeking; past performance becomes of secondary importance.

* Planning shall be a creative process — not filling in forms for Headquarters.

* The process of planning is a key issue emphasizing the teamwork aspect and integration of plans.

* Objective-oriented plans are motivating — we know what is expected from us — and provide for justice in performance appraisal and reward.

---

*Exhibit 11.* The scope of business.

| Technology/Products / Markets | Existing | Related | New |
|---|---|---|---|
| New | Services and know-how based on the skills and knowledge possessed within the Group | | Nonrelated new business |
| Related | Products manufactured to a quality and performance well suited to a particular market or market segment | Products based on technical skills and know-how possessed within the Group, which result in the products being superior or unique in performance or market requirements | |
| Existing | EXISTING BUSINESS<br>Rolling Bearings<br>Steel<br>Machinery<br>Tools<br>Textile Components<br>Other | Products with an advanced degree of technological sophistication | Products (manufactured or purchased) or services for which the Group possesses valuable marketing know-how and which can be channeled through the existing sales organization |

*Exhibit 12.*

| GROUP OBJECTIVES | COMPANY OBJECTIVES |
|---|---|
| *Group Purpose* | *Company Purpose* |
| Scope of business | Scope of business |
| Corporate identity | Role within the group |
| Social responsibility | Social responsibility |
| *Economic Objectives* | *Economic Objectives* |
| Internal control | Financial development |
| Related new business | Internal control |
| | Related new business |
| *Growth Strategy* | *Growth Strategy* |
| Improving existing business | Product/market strategy |
| Research and development | Improving existing business |
| Acquisitions | Research and development |
| Divestments | Acquisitions |
| | Divestments |

*Exhibit 13.* The SKF planning procedure.

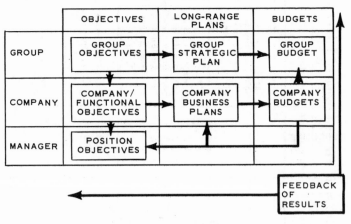

**Exhibit 14.** The corporate planning process in the SKF Group. The ultimate goal.

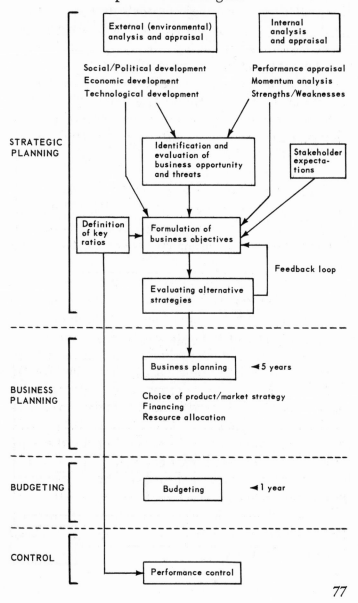

## Key Results Analysis

No matter how good the company's strategic and tactical plans, they are sterile until each manager has agreed with his boss on just what *his* results are to be and how these fit in with wider objectives.

So the manager wants agreement on what are the Key Results of his job. He wants a summary of its purpose, to know the Key Results to be achieved to fulfill this purpose, the performance standards and control methods which relate to the Key Results, and what limitations there are on his authority.

An extract from various Key Results Analyses is shown as Exhibit 15. Note that the manager's position in the organization and his personal activities are included. The heart of the analysis is of course the column on Key Tasks.

The manager also wants an Improvement Plan— that is, a plan to improve the basic results which integrates with a broader Improvement Plan for the unit.

This approach is much deeper and sharper than traditional lists of duties and responsibilities which are usually generalized and lengthy rather than specific, and which may confuse the manager's activities with the end result of these activities. At higher levels particularly, this confusion is inhibiting. Moreover, such statements invariably do not differentiate the vital profit-influencing elements from the trivial, and may crystallize the present without providing impetus for future improvement.

The difference between a traditional job description and a Key Results Analysis of the same job is shown in Exhibits 16 and 17.

*Exhibit 15.* Key Results Analysis.

| KEY TASK | PERFORMANCE STANDARD | CONTROL DATA | SUGGESTIONS FOR IMPROVEMENT |
|---|---|---|---|
| EXAMPLE OF A KEY TASK FOR A PRODUCTION MANAGER. Use of resources. To ensure that the most effective use is made of available resources. | LABOR:<br>When average waiting time never exceeds 0.5% in any month.<br>When ratio of direct to indirect labor does not exceed 4.0.<br>When labor turnover, including staff, does not exceed 15% p.a.<br>When pay performance is 95%.<br>MACHINES:<br>Average machine utilization never falls below 75%.<br>No machine is utilized for less than 65% of its time.<br>FLOOR SPACE:<br>When not less than 90% of available factory floor area is utilized for production.<br>STOCKS:<br>When the money utilized in providing stocks never exceeds the specified figure. | Returns from payroll office<br>Quarterly check on personnel records<br>Quarterly check on personnel records<br>Returns from payroll office<br>No control information available at present<br>No control information available at present<br>Annual check on floor area by plant engineer<br>Monthly accounts | This information must be produced.<br><br>These figures are based only on past experience; suggest a project be carried out to determine optimum figures. |
| EXAMPLE OF A KEY TASK FOR AN AREA SALES MANAGER. To establish with each customer the stock levels he should hold so that delivery times can be kept economic with minimum risk of stock-out. | Following delivery times are acceptable to customers and met<br><br>|  | 90% ORDERS WITHIN | 97% ORDERS WITHIN |<br>| CAT. 'A': | 7 days | 14 days |<br>| CAT. 'B': | 4 days | 7 days |<br>| Sp. Accts.: | 7 days | 14 days | | (1) Outstanding orders analysis<br><br>(2) Customer complaints | If we are to meet even these generous delivery times reliably, either depot stocks of some items will have to be increased or lead times from the factory reduced. I suggest an OR investigation of optimum stock levels. |
| EXAMPLE OF A KEY TASK FOR A RESEARCH MANAGER. To recognize competitors' technological strategy and to advise M.D. when objectives should be modified. | Company's marketing and operating programs never require crash changes due to failure to recognize competitors' technological strategy. | No record needed. Any such occurrence will be recognized by all. | Our methods of collecting news of competitors' technological strategy need improving. (See improvement plan for first half of 1972.) |

***Exhibit 16.*** Traditional job description for sales manager, medium-size furniture company.

*Position:* Sales Manager
*Responsible to:* The Managing Director
*Responsible for:* Representatives and Area Agents, Showroom, and Office Staff

The following terms of reference are not exclusive and certain items require effective delegation in whole or in part to be adequately fulfilled.

1. Advise and assist the Managing Director regarding sales and trading policy. Provide information on marketing trends and sales activity by maintaining an adequate system of information by the systematic collection of information on company activity from other sources he may select or be directed to use.

2. Maintain close consultation with the Director of Design and Development regarding the range, style, and quality of company products.

3. Process complaints by prompt attention, careful analysis, and participation in the product development committee to assist the elimination of defect when possible.

4. Vet incoming orders to clarify instructions and ensure through participation in the weekly production meetings that a system of priorities and questions relating to distribution are efficiently resolved.

5. Assume responsibility for the planning and organization of stock shows and ensure within the budget allowed for this activity that the maximum return is achieved from each show.

6. Assume responsibility for the initial selection of, the recommendations on the commission for, and the review of the activities of each agent or company representative.

7. Consult with the Managing Director on the appointment and dismissal of company agents or representatives and ensure that there is adequate information as to their performance against annual targets which are to be reviewed at least annually.

8. Assume responsibility for visiting all agents at least twice a year; ensure that these employees are given every opportunity to succeed by the provision of marketing devices, information, and general encouragement.

80

*Exhibit 16 — continued*

9. Ensure that the agents or representatives have up-to-date information on company products and the sales policy.

10. Maintain and review sources of market research information.

11. Assume responsibility for the effective administration of the processing of customers' orders and their progress to the point of invoicing.

12. Review the price structure of company products and make recommendations to the board in the light of manufacturing costs, material costs, demand for specialty including obsolescent styles, special dimensions, or special cloth, and changes in general consumer demands.

13. Contribute to the production development committee work on the reduction of variety and of manufacturing cost.

14. In general, keep price levels under continuous review in order to assess their competitiveness and profitability.

15. Consult with the Director of Design and Development before confirming orders for special one-of designs.

16. Prepare marketing publications and arrange for advertising; review the effectiveness of the company's advertising and public relations consultants.

17. Ensure that the staff employed in the office and the representatives and agents receive adequate training both internally and externally and arrange the preparation of his deputy to act for him in his absence and to prepare for his succession.

18. Liaise with the company's accountant on questions of customer credit and special billing arrangements that may be required.

19. Assume responsibility for the layout, cleanliness, and supervision of the permanent showroom.

20. Ensure that the company's design consultants are kept informed of any amendments to the schedule of stock and any special design requirements brought to his attention by the company's customers.

SOURCE: Furniture & Timber Industry Training Board, England.

*Exhibit 17.* Job description, Key Results Analysis, for sales manager, medium-size furniture company.

*Position:* Sales Manager
*Responsible to:* The Managing Director

*Subordinates directly supervised:*
Representatives and Area Agents; Office Staff; Showroom Staff

*Main purpose of job:*
To ensure the continued sales of the company's products to the agreed standards and to advise the Managing Director of the market environment surrounding these problems.

| Key Task | Standard of Performance | Review Information |
|---|---|---|
| 1<br>To ensure the company obtains its budgeted turnover and standard gross profit (excluding sales variances) | (1) The value of orders received does not fall below £x per week | Monthly analysis sheets |
| | (2) The average selling price of suites, other than sale lines, does not fall below the budgeted price for the period by more than 5% | Monthly analysis sheets |
| | (3) Cover sales do not fall below an average of £3,000 for each 3-month period. | Monthly analysis sheets |
| | (4) No locality within area fails by more than 5% to achieve the required volume and value in each 3-month period. | Monthly analysis sheets |
| | (5) Average budgeted gross profit of £x per suite does not fall by more than 1% due to change of product mix. | Monthly analysis sheets |
| 2<br>To maintain customers' goodwill | (1) All enquiries are actioned within 2 days and orders acknowledged within 3 days of receipt. | Weekly spot check |
| | (2) Delivery promises to be met in 90% of cases. Remaining 10% to be not less than 10 working days after promised date. | Order book and delivery schedules |
| | (3) All complaints acknowledged within 2 days. | Customer complaint and rep. call sheets |
| | (4) Services and sales aids to meet the needs specified on the customer record cards. | Customer record cards |

| Key Task | Standard of Performance | Review Information |
|---|---|---|
| **3**<br>To ensure effective consultation with Design, Production, and Accounting | **Design**<br>(1) Report details of all products introduced by 24 largest competitors within one month (including selling times quarterly) of appearance in the shops. | Dated report |
| | (2) Brief of new designs 9 months before required date. | Dated brief |
| | **Production**<br>(3) Quarterly forecast by products given within 3 days of end of each month. | Dated forecast |
| | **Accounts**<br>(4) Credit limits and terms agreed with Company Secretary before orders are processed. | Customer records |
| | (5) Overdue accounts settled within x weeks of delivery. | List of debtors |
| **4**<br>To advise Managing Director of present and projected market trends | (1) 12-month product forecast updated quarterly and submitted to Managing Director within 10 days of end of each period. | Dated forecast |
| | (2) Advise Managing Director of market reaction to present prices and movement of competitive prices quarterly. | Dated report |
| **5**<br>To ensure the organization of the department meets the requirements of the marketing function within the agreed indirect expenditure | (1) Representation is such as to achieve x calls per month on A accounts, y calls on B accounts, and z calls on C accounts. | Call sheets |
| | (2) Sales Manager to visit 35 customers each 3-month period. | Monthly report |
| | (3) No shortfall in standards of performance for any staff for more than two performance reviews. | Performance reviews |
| | (4) Overhead of Sales Department does not exceed budget. | Monthly profit and loss account |

SOURCE: Furniture & Timber Industry Training Board, England.

There is a general belief that managers know what is
expected of them even though it may not be written
down. "After all," said one general manager of his plant
manager, "he's been doing the job for eight years. If he
doesn't know what is expected of him by now, what
have I been paying him for?"

In practice we find that many managers are unclear
as to which results are important. These gray areas are
a potent cause of personal insecurity and conservatism.
Wilfred Brown points out that "If every time a manager
faces a problem his first thought is 'Is it my responsibility to deal with this or not?' then a state of uncertainty
develops which often impedes initiative." [14]

Our experience is supported by research. When
N. F. Maier and L. R. Hoffman of the University of
Michigan conducted detailed interviews with 222 managerial pairs, as part of a study of differences in job per-
ception between boss and subordinate, only 8.1 percent
showed almost complete agreement. [15]

In relation to obstacles in the way of effective subordinate performance there was almost complete disagreement on obstacles in 38.6 percent of the pairs.

## KEY TASKS AND PERFORMANCE STANDARDS

To distinguish whether a key task is *really* important, we should ask, with Drucker:

> In what areas would excellence really have an ex-
> traordinary impact on the economic results of our busi-
> ness, to the point where it might transform the eco-
> nomic performance of the entire business? . . . In

what areas would poor performance threaten to damage economic performance, greatly or at least significantly? [16]

Key Tasks and performance standards must be consistent within a company, but unfortunately parochialism can often be seen. For example, a production unit which sets a higher quality standard without reference to the market standard as seen by the sales department may be pursuing an apparently worthy aim which is not in the wider company interest.

The best way to ensure that there is a proper integration between key areas of the business and Key Tasks of the individual manager is to use the matrix analysis referred to earlier.

For each Key Task there must be an indication of performance standards. By performance standard we mean a statement of conditions which exist when the result is being satisfactorily achieved. It is not a statement of the ideal results in ideal circumstances nor the minimum acceptable standard.

Performance standards are of two main categories:

*Measured,* or quantitative, standards can be expressed in terms such as goods produced per month, cost levels, market penetration per product, percent delay time, or ratios of return on investment.

*Judged,* or qualitative, standards, although not directly measurable in quantitative terms, can be verified by judgment and observation. For example: "Key results analysis and improvement plans prepared for all immediate subordinates and revised annually."

Wherever possible, quantitative standards are sought. Often these can be developed in areas where at first sight only subjective opinions appear to be available. Many such standards already exist in a business through budgets, allocations, technical specifications, and so on; in this case the value is to integrate them with key results and controls, perhaps for the first time. The analysis may reveal key areas where no standards at present exist.

Clearly these performance standards relate to the job, not the jobholder, and if they are not met, it is a cue for the manager's superior to take constructive action by retraining, removing obstacles to successful performance, or re-deploying the manager to more suitable work. Poor standards can often be detected by observing the use of such comfortable words as adequate, approximately, few, as soon as possible, reasonable, minimum, desirable.

Some examples of performance standards are given in Exhibit 18.

### THE NEED TO INVOLVE MANAGERS

It is possible that an analysis of this kind *could* be made by a skilled analyst, but it would be contrary to the whole concept of MBO. The manager must make his own analysis—the adviser or "change agent" is merely fulfilling a coaching or catalyst role, not making the definition. Unless the manager is motivated to look critically at his job; unless he feels confident that he has the support of his boss when they talk it through together; unless he has opportunities to work in a team with colleagues on the interlocking problems, all that will be produced is a piece of paper. The real meaning of MBO is a deep involvement which releases the creative ideas within each man.

86

Invariably many improvement ideas emerge. These are typical:

"Our industrial relations policy is not clear and inhibits decisions."

"We need to make a market study for Product X."

"Control data for machine shop utilization is not satisfactory."

"It appears that four levels of supervision are not necessary and we should now make a detailed study to recast the structure with three levels."

"We need to revise the present staff report forms."

A critical analysis of these problems is often fruitful and leads to the buildup of individual improvement plans designed to overcome the difficulties.

## IMPROVEMENT PLANS

The Key Results Analysis provides an excellent framework for the continuing results a manager must achieve, but he also requires a short-term Improvement Plan which focuses his immediate effort on matters of dominant company importance. The manager commits himself to achieving Key Results and Improvement Plan Results; both are necessary.

## WHOSE RESPONSIBILITY?

It is the manager's responsibility to reach agreement with his immediate subordinate managers on analysis of their Key Results and short-term Improvement Plans; in turn these are reviewed and approved by the manager's own boss. Where there are problems, incompatible standards, or opportunities which impinge on more than

*Exhibit 18.* Examples of performance standards and review information, middle manager.

| Key Task | Possible Performance Standards | Review Information |
|---|---|---|
| SALES AND MARKETING<br>Forecasting sales | (a) Forecasts of 75% of models are within 10% of actual sales.<br>(b) Forecasts for remaining 25% are within 50% of actuals. | Monthly sales analysis |
| Selling | (a) Achieve the sales targets set, i.e., obtain £x,000 of orders each month.<br>(b) The gross sales margins are not less than: (1) Product A, 40%; (2) Product B, 25%.<br>(c) Price reviews are held quarterly. | Monthly sales analysis<br><br>Monthly sales analysis |
| Development of business | (a) The x most important customers are identified and called on at least y times a year.<br>(b) At least z new customers place an order in each 6 months. | Call records<br>Monthly order book |
| Market standing | (a) x% of the UK market share is maintained for product Category A.<br>(b) A y% increase in the UK market share is achieved for product Category B. | Monthly orders and BOT/statistics<br>BOT/Association statistics |
| Management of sales force | Key results agreed with each manager and reviewed and updated quarterly. | Annual review |
| PRODUCTION<br>Scheduling production to meet agreed delivery dates | 95% of orders completed by forecast date. | Record of delivery dates, forecast and actual |
| Maintaining quality standards | (a) Not more than 3% of finished products returned from final inspection.<br>(b) No justified complaint from customer due to quality below standard. | Weekly inspection reports<br>Analysis of customer returns |

| Key Task | Possible Performance Standards | Review Information |
|---|---|---|
| Effective use of labor | (a) 90% of labor to be on measured work. | Time sheets |
| | (b) Average performance to be 95% under the bonus scheme. | Time sheets |
| | (c) Overtime working to meet weekly planned programs. | Weekly programs and overtime records |
| | (d) Labor turnover, including staff, not exceeding 25% p.a. | Quarterly check on personnel records |
| Obtaining maximum machine utilization | (a) Average machine utilization never below x%. | Weekly "lost time" and breakdown records |
| Reducing waste | (a) Waste does not exceed x% on softwood, y% on hardwood, z% on veneers, etc. | Weekly consolidation of daily checks |
| | (b) Material usage does not exceed budgeted figures. | Monthly account |
| Stock control | (a) Stocks do not exceed budgeted figure. | Monthly account |
| Recognizing new techniques | Company's program never requires crash changes due to failure to recognize better techniques. | No record needed |
| ADMINISTRATION | | |
| Implementing company policy on employment | No dispute causing stoppage due to the manager's method of applying company policy. | No record necessary |
| Ensuring safety standards are maintained | (a) No accident due to regulations not being observed or operator not using correct method of working. | Accident reports |
| | (b) Total accident rate not to exceed x%. | Accident reports |
| Controlling debtors | Debts outstanding at the end of each month do not exceed the amount of the previous 6 weeks' invoicing. | Monthly accounts |

SOURCE: Furniture & Timber Industry Training Board, England.

one man, groups will meet to thrash out together the best solution. Thus there is:

The fullest opportunity for three levels of management to make a constructive contribution.

Less danger of low or unrealistic standards being developed, or prejudice creeping in.

Teamwork in solving common problems.

A wider view taken of individual and departmental objectives to confirm that they are directed to company goals.

Exhibits 19 and 20 illustrate vividly the educational process in these discussions and show how a manager's first attempt at an Improvement Plan was clarified and linked with company priorities by discussion.

Should a manager disagree with his superior, the superior must, of course, retain the right to have his way. In practice this occurs infrequently. Where the right climate of opinion has been created, both men are sincerely searching for the truth and accept the "law of the situation."

### *Performance Review and Potential Review*

When reviewing the manager, we differentiate Performance Review and Potential Review:

#### PERFORMANCE REVIEW

The manager's superior analyzes how well the Key Results and Improvement Plan have been met and dis-

*Exhibit 19.* Improvement Plan, first attempt.

Period _____ to _____

Submitted By AREA MANAGER _____ Date _____

| KEY TASK NO. | OBJECTIVE OR STANDARD | PERSONAL ACTION PLANNED | COMMENCEMENT/COMPLETION DATES | DATES ACTION TAKEN | COMMENTS – including reasons for action not taken, changes in plan |
|---|---|---|---|---|---|
| 1 | Achieve sales target | Concentrate on specific product groups. Direct mail scheme. | | | |
| 3 | Control area credit | Discuss with representatives. | | | |
| 4 | Improve knowledge of area market | Each representative to compile customer records. | | | |
| 5 | Improve area coverage | As above. Supervise callage plans. | | | |
| 7 | Development of representatives | Work out quarterly targets. Hold meetings at regular intervals. | | | |
| 8 | Personal selling | Maintain contact with major accounts. | | | |

*Exhibit 20.* Improvement Plan, second attempt.

Period 1ST JANUARY, 1972 to 31ST MARCH, 1972
Submitted By AREA MANAGER    Date 7TH JANUARY, 1972

| KEY TASK NO. | OBJECTIVE OR STANDARD | PERSONAL ACTION PLANNED | COMMENCE-MENT/ COMPLETION DATES | DATES ACTION TAKEN | COMMENTS — including reasons for action not taken, changes in plan |
|---|---|---|---|---|---|
| 1 | 1) Achieve dairy foods sales target for 1st quarter<br><br>2) Achieve pig food sales target for 1972 | (a) Personal assistance to representatives Smith and Brown with 4 large dairy prospects.<br>(b) Attend 2 Inglenook meetings.<br>(c) Plan pig food sales drive for April-June quarter.<br>(d) Hold area meeting to discuss strategy and hold preliminary briefing. | JAN. 31<br><br>JAN. 31<br>FEB. 29<br>MAR. 15 | | |
| 2 | Minimize costs | Hold area meeting on subject of minimizing costs and reducing credit, Jones to lead discussion on reduction of credit. | JAN. 31 | | |
| 3 | Control area credit | Representatives Black and White to be instructed in cash collection procedures. Personal collection of arrears from customers slow and tardy. | FEB. 29 | | |
| 4 | Develop knowledge of area market | Complete customer record cards for 60% of area.<br>Complete prospect cards for 25% of area. | MAR. 31<br>MAR. 31 | | |
| 5 | Improve area coverage | Callage plans completed for Smith, Brown, Black, White, and Grey. | MAR. 31 | | |

cusses success and failure. He will, of course, have been doing this in detail as an integral part of his daily management job. A formal review is, however, an essential discipline for creating a sense of accountability in both manager and superior in a broader sense than is possible in day-to-day management. It ensures that every manager is systematically thought about as an individual in his own right.

The review demonstrates gaps in knowledge and skills which can be filled by planned guidance and training. It is the occasion when the Key Results Analysis is brought up to date and a new Improvement Plan is settled; thus it is positive, not negative, in spirit, seeking to provide change for the better in job and man. It is much better if the jobholder takes the initiative in discussing results at the review.

## POTENTIAL REVIEW

The manager's potential is then considered by his superior and others, such as the personnel manager. Should he be moved to different types of work? Is he ready for promotion now? Is there some indication that he should be given accelerated opportunities? Closely linked with this aspect of review is the type of guidance he will need for the next stage in his career.

Although the Potential Review is made at the same time as the Performance Review and is obviously influenced by it, the range of factors considered is wider and more subjective.

## REVIEW DISCUSSIONS

The manager's superior may seek informally the opinion of other people at his own status level where they have had a direct working relationship with the manager concerned and can contribute. The responsibility for the final Review is absolutely that of the manager's superior.

To minimize prejudice and bias, the superior must in turn discuss with *his* boss the completed reviews.

Finally—and of vital importance—the manager and superior *must* meet to discuss to what extent the Key Results and Improvement Plan were met, what obstacles and difficulties emerged, and to positively shape together the next Improvement Plan. Where it is likely to be fruitful and constructive, certain parts of the Potential Review are also discussed. However, the wider discussion on the man's future might be held with him at a higher level, with his superior's full knowledge.

### DOUBTS ABOUT PERFORMANCE REVIEW

While the review or appraisal of managers is a logical and essential feature of any program of management development, there is persistent controversy about methods and value.

A European study [17] of six companies and 1,440 manager appraisals was made to find out how appraisal procedures work in practice, and three main conclusions were reached:

1. *Appraisers are reluctant to appraise*
   They do not always complete forms when required to do so; they do not always complete every section of the form as required; they do not always acknowledge authorship; the content of the entry is often evasive.

2. *Interviewers are even more reluctant to interview*

### 3. The follow-up is inadequate

Managers who find that reports carry little or no weight when transfers, promotion, or training are considered are unlikely to attach much importance to their completion. This attitude is encouraged when the person to whom the reports go is prepared to accept incomplete or inadequate reports without question.

Similar disappointment is reported [18] from some divisions in General Electric, which is highly regarded for its progressive management policies and methods. Robert L. Miles, of its Flight Propulsion Division, found in one division that appraisals were divorced from results. In a second, preoccupation with personality factors ("imaginative," "creative," "lots of drive") led to high ratings which were of little value when the division came under competitive pressure. In the Small Aircraft Engine Department, the company collaborated with the University of Michigan's Institute for Social Research and discovered that appraisal discussions were not effective in getting people to change; they were "so full of generalities they were easily forgotten" and the managers said that they wanted some specific goals.

The late Douglas McGregor believed that the wrong type of appraisal is positively harmful, not merely unhelpful. He wrote:

> The conventional approach, unless handled with consummate skill and delicacy, constitutes something close to a violation of the integrity of the personality.
> Managers are uncomfortable when they are put in the position of playing God. The respect we hold for

the inherent value of the individual leaves us distressed when we must take the responsibility for judging the personal worth of a fellow man.

Yet the conventional approach to performance appraisal forces us not only to make such judgments and to see them acted upon, but also to communicate them to those we have judged. Small wonder we resist.[19]

Kay Rowe, who led the European study, is also positive:

> . . . no appraiser has the moral right to pass judgment on such qualities, except in so far as they are directly and demonstrably relevant in the subordinate's job. Obviously personality is important in any job but the appraiser has no right to pass judgment on personality; he can only judge performance.[20]

### SOME GUIDELINES FOR SUCCESSFUL REVIEW

Clearly many of these doubts spring from a failure to identify from the beginning an understood and agreed-upon base against which the manager is going to be reviewed. An overpreoccupation with personality also causes suspicion. The need to carry out reviews remains, and in our experience the following guidelines are helpful:

*Concentrate on performance rather than personality.* Of course personality is important. However, there is no agreement that a personality profile for a successful manager exists, and if it did, how could we define it in terms the layman can understand? Where does one draw the line, for example, between self-confidence and aggressiveness? Moreover, this emphasis is usually unconstructive in that it is difficult to train or develop a mature person's personality and it is often a genuine embarrassment for the superior to attempt to discuss this with him.

To stress the use a man *makes* of his personality in achieving results is more helpful to him and to the company. It leads to the identification of job performance obstacles and gaps in personal knowledge on which action can be taken.

*Concentrate on action for improvement.* The review should be regarded not as a somewhat negative tool of personnel administration but as a stimulus for improving the man's future performance and the results of the job itself. The discussions should always be forward looking rather than just an inquest on the past.

*Encourage genuine participation—let the jobholder take the initiative.* Managers are usually suspicious and cynical about reviews of a traditional kind. They accept readily reviews concerned mainly with measuring success against an objective base which they had a share in creating. In Rensis Likert's words:

> People seem most willing and emotionally able to accept, and to examine in a nondefensive manner, information about themselves and their behavior, including their inadequacies, when it is in the form of *objective* evidence.[21]

It is much better for the manager himself to analyze his success and failure than for the boss to dominate in this review.

Discussions with superiors are welcomed also as an opportunity to bring the Key Results Analysis up to date and work out the next Improvement Plan. The knowledge that possible prejudice is minimized by this more objective base of Key Results and that the reviews are reviewed by his superior's boss further encourages a manager's support.

*Keep review in the line.* It is the personal and undelegatable responsibility of every manager to review the performance of his subordinates. Done properly this strengthens the quality of relationship between manager and subordinate. Unless this is understood, the reviews and discussions may be viewed as "optional extras" or an extra burden. At the *introduction* of reviews, an adviser plays a useful role in counseling people in the method, often by sitting in on review discussions. This is a temporary, not permanent, role. The company personnel specialists make a continuing contribution in advising line managers which are the best methods of review and assisting in administration. They also provide such support as training facilities. It is never their responsibility to review performance except that of their own staff.

*Distinguish Performance and Potential Reviews.* It is best to separate the mechanics of Performance and Potential Reviews even though they are made at the same time.

Performance Review can be discussed fully and jointly by the manager and his superior; the Potential Review may contain views and judgments about the future which it may be unhelpful to discuss completely with the manager at that state. The superior's boss may discuss the manager's long-term future directly with him.

It must be admitted that we know little about potential; indeed, the best single predictor of a man's future success as a manager appears to be past success in similar kinds of managerial work. We can always reassure ourselves with Jean Cocteau's thought: "There must be such a thing as luck. How else can one account for the success of one's enemies?"

*Let Performance Review influence Salary Review indirectly.* In practice, salary levels can, and must, be influenced by factors other than performance alone. It is also certain that, when salary recommendations are directly included, the constructive nature of review discussions is impaired. The ideal solution appears to be to consider salary recommendations within a month or two of Performance Review while the influence is still strong.

Our experience is supported by Kay Rowe's research. She concludes that the appraisal procedure should have no explicit connection with Salary Review: "It would, of course, be illogical if there were wide discrepancies between appraisal and salary review, but the two should be regarded as separate activities." Another General Electric study of their performance appraisal methods reported,

> One of the first interesting things was that as soon as the manager raised the question of dollars, the constructive attitude immediately left the room. Both the manager and the individual appeared to go on the defensive.[22]

The link between material rewards and Performance Review will become much closer as we are able to measure important results more accurately and when the habit of setting objectives and frankly reviewing progress is established.

A "high reward/high contribution" outlook is built

99

into management by objectives. Provided the methods of remuneration are professionally sound, this philosophy supports other powerful motivators such as recognition, personal contribution and achievement, and the challenge of the work itself.

*Provide training in coaching and counseling.* We have found that the review process goes much better when people have been given an opportunity to learn and practice coaching and counseling skills.

To sum up: Performance and Potential Reviews are vital parts of a management by objectives program. They provide a frank discussion between manager and superior on:

Did we achieve the key results of this job?
Did we succeed in meeting the targets of the Improvement Plan?
Do we need to revise the Key Results Analysis?
What are the priorities for improvement in the future?

Moreover, it is the raw material from which worthwhile training programs and succession plans are built.

### Management Training

Management training is the process of developing managers' knowledge, skills, and attitudes through instruction, demonstration, practice, and planned experience to meet the present and future needs of the business and of the manager. This is a vast subject in its own right, but some general guidelines can be given.

Exhibit 21 illustrates a systematic way to build the company training plan. The weaknesses which hinder a man from getting good results on his present job are identified as a by-product of Performance Review. Potential Review will indicate the new skills and knowledge required by the man for the next job he might occupy. Finally, top management and its staff advisers consider any additional training needs arising, for example, from strategic plans, changes in technology, new methods, and so on. Many companies rush prematurely into training activity without being sure what the real needs are, and this shot-gun approach is costly and ineffective.

One training manager set up short courses on human relations because he felt it was an obvious need. Later Performance Review showed that the real priorities were a better grasp of labor cost control and a refresher course on some technical aspects of the work.

The analysis of needs is best done by the manager and his superior with professional support from the personnel or training officer.

### CONCENTRATE ON ON-THE-JOB TRAINING

The major influence on a man's development is what happens on the job—the demanding nature of his responsibilities and the guidance of his boss. Every manager has an undelegatable and continuing responsibility to develop and train himself and his subordinates.

This on-the-job training may often be informal in method, but it must be planned in relation to a man's needs and followed up regularly.

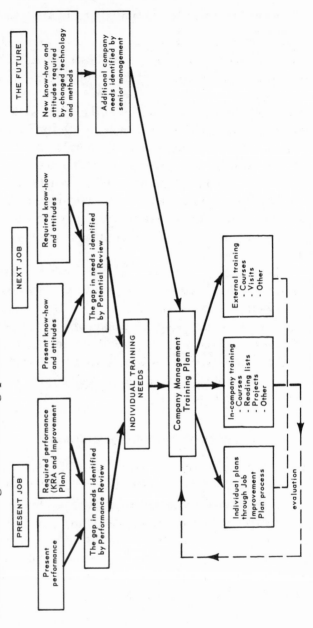

*Exhibit 21.* Management training process.

Some companies use an individual training plan as a memory jog. It just records the need, what is to be taught, by whom, and by when. A very simple example for a cost accountant might take the form shown in Exhibit 22.

On-the-job training has its limitations. Pressure of daily work constantly pushes training into second place,

*Exhibit 22.* Individual training plan.

NAME: **MICHAEL PALMER**     DEPT. **FINANCIAL**
POSITION HELD: **FACTORY COST ACCOUNTANT**
APPRAISAL FINDINGS: **REQUIRES TRAINING IN DCF ANALYSIS**

TRAINING OBJECTIVES:

1. Explain basic principles of market forecasting techniques

2. Interpret forecasts in terms of cash flow statements

3. Relate forecasts to customers and markets served by Electronery

**EVALUATION BY ASSIGNMENT.**

SIGNED: _____

no matter how good intentions are. Moreover, some managers get poor guidance from bosses who cannot teach, or who themselves are out of date, or who are too insecure personally to wish to pass on their experience.

Job rotation is a popular form of on-the-job training. Sometimes it is abused when the man is an observer or supernumerary with no weight of personal responsibility, or when the job is held for so short a time that efficiency suffers and the man never stays anywhere long enough for retribution to catch up with him! It can also pose a dilemma: should we encourage this manager to become a real expert in his subject or should we move him about to create the rounded experience for general management appointments? A sound job rotation scheme, where responsible work is carried out in a series of planned appointments designed to fit the man's career pattern, can make an important contribution.

As L. F. Urwick puts it, "Doing jobs well, being encouraged to do jobs that are a little outside what he believes to be his strength and then succeeding at them," is a major influence on a man's development.

### CONSIDER THE INDIVIDUAL BEFORE THE GROUP NEED

There are as many training "problems" as there are individual managers. This concern with the individual does not, of course, lead to the neglect of training needs arising from his role as a member of a team. Management training must help a man to work effectively on project teams, committees, study groups, and so on, which are of growing importance as business grows in complexity. Training in the context of management by objectives must be a dynamic approach to the *individual's* needs and his wider needs as a member of the management *team*.

Earlier in this book an effective method of group training has been described. For personal training and development, these methods should be considered:

Job rotation
Guided reading
A period as personal assistant to a senior manager
Special personal project
Membership of a committee
Attendance at conferences
Encouragement to participate in outside activities, such as Chamber of Commerce, management institute, trade associations
Attendance at a selected outside course

### USE A WIDE RANGE OF TEACHING METHODS

Companies become over-dedicated to one method when in fact there is a wide range to choose from. Examine the list in Exhibit 23, which is intended only as a general guide to those most commonly used.

### MAKE GOOD USE OF IN-COMPANY COURSES

When a pattern of common needs arises, often the most convenient and efficient solution is to run an internal training course. The proven needs will determine the basic content. Imaginative and professional advice from, for example, the personnel officer, on *how* to present the material, or on what are the most suitable teaching aids, is a great advantage. It is also valuable

*Exhibit* 23. A brief guide to training techniques.

| METHOD | WHAT IT IS | WHAT IT WILL ACHIEVE | POINTS TO WATCH |
|--------|-----------|---------------------|-----------------|
| Lecture | A talk given without much, if any, participation in the form of questions or discussion on the part of the trainees. | Suitable for large audiences where participation of the trainees is not possible because of numbers. The information to be put over can be exactly worked out beforehand, even to the precise word. The timing can be accurately worked out. | The lack of participation on the part of the audiences means that unless the whole of it, from beginning to end, is fully understood and assimilated the sense will be lost. |
| Talk | A talk incorporating a variety of techniques, and allowing for participation by the trainees. The participation may be in the form of questions asked of trainees, their questions to the speaker, or brief periods of discussion during the session. | Suitable for putting across information to groups of not more than twenty trainees. Participation by the trainees keeps their interest and helps them to learn. | The trainees have the opportunity to participate but may not wish to do so. The communication will then be all one way and the session will be little different from a lecture. |

| METHOD | WHAT IT IS | WHAT IT WILL ACHIEVE | POINTS TO WATCH |
|---|---|---|---|
| Job (Skill) Instruction | A session during which a job or part of a job is learned according to the following formula:<br>a. The trainee is told how to do the job.<br>b. The trainee is shown how to do the job.<br>c. The trainee does the job under supervision.<br><br>Each of these parts may be a complete session in itself:<br>a. Talk<br>b. Demonstration<br>c. Practice | Suitable for putting across skills. The job is broken down into small stages which are practiced. The whole skill is thus built up in easily understood stages. This gives the trainees confidence and helps them to learn.<br><br>More suitable when the skill to be learned is one which depends on a lot of knowledge first being learned. Many clerical skills are of this sort. | The skills to be acquired may best be learned as a whole rather than as parts.<br><br>It is difficult for trainees to absorb large chunks of information and then to be shown what to do at some length before they get the opportunity to put the learning into practice. |
| Discussion | Knowledge, ideas, and opinions on a particular subject are freely exchanged among the trainees and with the instructor. | Suitable where the application of information is a matter of opinion. Also when attitudes need to be induced or changed. Trainees are more likely to change attitudes after discussion than they would if they were told during a talk that their attitude should be changed. Also suitable as a means of obtaining feedback to the instructor about the way in which trainees may apply the knowledge learned. | The trainees may stray from the subject matter or fail to discuss it usefully. The whole session may be blurred and woolly. Trainees may become firmer in their attitudes rather than more prepared to change them. |

*Exhibit 23 – continued*

| METHOD | WHAT IT IS | WHAT IT WILL ACHIEVE | POINTS TO WATCH |
|---|---|---|---|
| Role Playing | Trainees are asked to enact, in the training situation, the role they will be called upon to play in their job or work. Used mainly for the practice of dealing with face-to-face situations (i.e., where people come together in the work situation). | Suitable where the subject is one where a near-to-life practice in the training situation is helpful to the trainees. The trainees can practice and receive expert advice or criticism and opinions of their colleagues in a protected training situation. This gives confidence as well as offering guidelines. The trainees get the feel of the pressures of the real-life situation. | Trainees may be embarrassed and their confidence sapped rather than built up. It can also be regarded as a bit of a lark and not taken seriously. |
| Case Study | A history of some event or set of circumstances, with the relevant details, is examined by the trainees. Case studies fall into two broad categories:<br>a. Those in which the trainees diagnose the causes of a particular problem.<br>b. Those in which the trainees set out to solve a particular problem. | Suitable where a cool look at the problem or set of circumstances, free from the pressures of the actual event, is beneficial. It provides opportunities for exchange of ideas and consideration of possible solutions to problems the trainees will face in the work situation. | Trainees may get the wrong impression of the real work situation. They may fail to realize that decisions taken in the training situations are different from those which have to be made on the spot in a live situation. |

| METHOD | WHAT IT IS | WHAT IT WILL ACHIEVE | POINTS TO WATCH |
|---|---|---|---|
| Exercise | Trainees are asked to undertake a particular task, leading to a required result, following lines laid down by the trainers. It is usually a practice or a test of knowledge put over prior to the exercise.<br><br>Exercises may be used to discover trainees' existing knowledge or ideas before further information or new ideas are introduced. Exercises may be posed for individuals or for groups. | Suitable for any situation where the trainees need to practice following a particular pattern or formula to reach a required objective. The trainees are to some extent on their own. This is a highly active form of learning.<br><br>Exercises are frequently used instead of formal tests to find out how much the trainee has assimilated. There is a lot of scope in this method for the imaginative trainer. | The exercise must be realistic and the expected result reasonably attainable by all trainees or the trainees will lose confidence and experience frustration. |
| Project | Similar to an exercise but giving the trainee much greater opportunity for the display of initiative and creative ideas. The particular task is laid down by the trainer but the lines to be followed to achieve the objectives are left to the trainee to decide. Like exercises, projects may be set for either individuals or groups. | Suitable where initiative and creativity need stimulating or testing.<br><br>Projects provide feedback on a range of personal qualities of trainees as well as their range of knowledge and attitude to the job. Like exercises, projects may be used instead of formal tests. Again there is a lot of scope for the imaginative trainer. | It is essential that the project be undertaken with the trainee full interest and cooperation. It must also be seen by the trainee to be directly relevant to his needs.<br><br>If the trainee fails, or feels he has failed, in the project there will be severe loss of confidence on his part and possible antagonism toward the trainer. Trainees are often hypersensitive to criticism of project work. |

*Exhibit 23 – concluded*

| METHOD | WHAT IT IS | WHAT IT WILL ACHIEVE | POINTS TO WATCH |
|---|---|---|---|
| In-box | Trainees are given a series of files, papers, and letters similar to those they will be required to deal with at the place of work (i.e. the typical content of a desk worker's in-box). Trainees take action on each piece of work. The results are marked or compared with one another. | Suitable for giving trainee desk workers a clear undertaking of the real-life problems and their solutions. The simulation of the real situation aids the transfer of learning from the training to the work situation.<br><br>A valuable way of obtaining feedback on the trainees' progress. Also useful for developing attitudes toward the work, e.g., priorities, customers' complaints, superiors, etc. | It is important that the contents of the in-box be realistic. The aim should be to provide trainees with a typical in-box. The marking or comparison of results must be done in a way which will not sap the confidence of the weaker trainee. |
| Business and Management Games | Trainees are presented with information about a company – financial position, products, markets, etc. They are given different management roles to perform. One group may be concerned with sales, another with production, and so on. | Suitable for giving trainee managers practice in dealing with management problems. The simulation of the real-life situation not only aids the transfer of learning but is necessary because a trainee manager applying only broad theoretical knowledge to the work situation could cause major problems. | The main difficulty is in assessing the probable results of the decisions made. Sometimes a computer is used for this purpose. The trainees may reject the whole of the learning if they feel the assessment of the probable outcome of their decisions is unrealistic. |

| METHOD | WHAT IT IS | WHAT IT WILL ACHIEVE | POINTS TO WATCH |
|---|---|---|---|
| Business and Management Games (continued) | These groups then "run" the company. Decisions are made and actions are taken. The probable result of these decisions in terms of profitability is then calculated. | It helps considerably in developing many aspects of a manager's role. Also a valuable way of assessing the potential and performance of trainees. | |
| Group Dynamics | Trainees are put into situations in which: a. The behavior of each individual in the group is subject to examination and comment by the other trainees. b. The behavior of the group (or groups) as a whole is examined. (The trainer is a psychologist, a sociologist, or person who has himself received special training.) | A vivid way for the trainee to learn of the effect of his behavior on other people and the effect of their behavior upon him. It increases knowledge of how and why people at work behave as they do. It increases skills of working with other people and of getting work done through other people. A valuable way of learning the skill of communication. | Difficulties can arise if what the trainee learns about himself is distasteful to him. Trainees may opt out if they feel put off by the searching examination of motives. It is important that problems arising within the group be resolved before the group breaks up. |

to involve senior managers—for example, in preparing and presenting a talk, leading a discussion, commenting on report-back sessions. The advantage of internal courses is that they can really fit the company's special needs and simulate in atmosphere and techniques what will happen back on the job.

Internal courses have disadvantages too. They can be *too* insular and company oriented; the required knowledge may not be available from within; smaller companies often have neither the time nor the resources to set up a course.

Remember that in-company courses:

*Can*
- be focused precisely on the company's problems and the needs of those attending;
- be related to real job problems so that the learning process is integrated with the "back home" application;
- give opportunities for senior managers to make a personal contribution to training;
- be arranged to suit the location and times of the group concerned;
- often be evaluated more satisfactorily in on-the-job forms.

*Cannot*
- provide the stimulus and learning experience which come from mixed company groups;
- always overcome the inhibitions and insularity of an internal activity;
- easily call on the widest range of professional expertise in all subjects;
- help the small company as much as the large one.

My colleague Edwin Singer, in his column in *Industrial Training International*,[23] summarizes his experience with tailor-made in-company courses:

"A number of progressive companies have come up with new ideas. They have started by considering the major problems of their company and arranged for the course leaders to observe managers in action before they attend the course. This observation is more than asking him a few questions about his learning needs. It involves spending a period of time with him, trying to understand his problems, and observing the effect of pressures on his performance.

"The next step is to draw up a syllabus of subject areas which are of importance to the company and to prepare some notes on each subject which are written specifically with the company's staff in mind. Tasks are selected which will be carried out by the course members. Each task is of value to the company, but is designed also to extend the manager in areas with which he is unfamiliar. The keynote of the preparation period, therefore, is personalizing the course for the benefit of the company and of the individual.

"The actual course program extends over a period of several weeks but managers attend only for one day each week. The rest of the time they get on with their ordinary work. Each session is run using discovery learning principles. Work problems are discussed in terms of the subject area under consideration. The course leader will give an input of technical information when requested to do so by the course members. The emphasis is on those attending learning from each other. The job of the course leader is crucial for success. He is a mentor and guide—not just a purveyor of information. Between sessions he will assist members with their tasks and discuss with them any personal difficulties they have in applying the concepts which have been discussed during the formal sessions.

"The benefits of this approach to in-company management training have been considerable. The performance of those attending has improved and they have shown a willingness to innovate. Communication across the companies has been strengthened and managers have gained understanding of each other's problems.

"The greatest benefit of all has been succinctly expressed by one manager who attended such a course:

> When I came on this course I expected to be told things I did not know. During it I discovered I knew a great deal, but did not know how to apply what I know in practice. The greatest benefit it has been is that I now have a clear idea of those things I must get to know more about.

"This is the key to successful in-plant management training. The end point of the course is the beginning of understanding by a man of what he needs to learn."

### USE OUTSIDE COURSES SELECTIVELY

An external course can help. There is the stimulus of meeting managers from other companies and industries; the knowledge ought to be up to date and professionally well presented; new ideas can be fed back into company experience. Major problems do arise. How does one choose *which* course to support when every day brings a new collection of persuasive brochures? If the need has been well defined, the best starting point for advice is the American Management Associations. At least this produces a short list of "possibles." It is a good investment then to visit the courses on this short list when courses are being run.

There are three important ways to make the best use of an external course:

1. *Clarify your need*

Just why are you looking for an outside course? Who will be attending? Is a course definitely the best solution?

2. *Check on the course*

Faced with a torrent of glossy brochures, be selective and critical. If possible visit the establishment. Anyway, be sure to ask questions like these:

- How long has this management training institution been in existence?
- What are the qualifications and experience of the staff and how long have they been there?
- What are the objectives of the courses offered and how will you evaluate whether these objectives have been reached?
- What are the teaching techniques used (lectures, case studies, business games, etc.), and what is the proportion of time spent on these?
- What notes or books are issued for permanent reference?
- How many men attend each course? On the last course what age, functions and positions, companies were represented?
- What are the administrative arrangements and costs (residential, meals, etc.)?

3. *Brief the manager*

Brief the selected candidate before he attends and discuss in detail what has been learned on his return. For example, the manager should know that he will be expected to write a paper after the course, answering the questions:

- What practical ideas/knowledge can be used in his job and elsewhere in the company?
- What is his frank assessment of the course's strengths and weaknesses? Would he recommend using it again?

### BUILD ON STRENGTHS

Training is often regarded in a negative way, as "overcoming" a manager's weaknesses. This is useful, but both the company and the man may find it more useful to concentrate on building up his demonstrated strengths and abilities.

### TRAIN FOR THE FUTURE AS WELL AS THE PRESENT

Forward company plans should always have associated with them a plan for creating the new knowledge or skills which will be required. One insurance company sent all managers on training courses with a computer manufacturer before the computer was installed. When a textile mill decided to re-equip with a new type of automatic loom, the weaving manager spent some months with the supplier studying the managerial as well as the technical implications of the equipment well *before* the looms were delivered.

### EVALUATE THE RESULTS OF TRAINING

Although it is difficult, and in some cases impossible, to evaluate the results of training, the effort is worthwhile.

The discipline of establishing from the beginning just what changes training is required to achieve often stems from the awareness that evaluation is going to be attempted. Even where its impact on the manager is hard to evaluate, much can be learned about the content, methods, and presentation of the training so that it can be improved next time.

As with all the other techniques we are discussing, training can make its full contribution only if it is part of the total process of improving performance. In isolation, it achieves little and may even be injurious to the business. The classic warning is contained in a study of a series of management training courses carried out in one company. These courses were professionally well conducted and welcomed by the staff who attended; unfortunately top management was not itself deeply involved in the training. It is reported that the company

> . . . did achieve participant attitude change but found that the new attitudes conflicted with the practices of top management.
>
> This conflict brought about serious organization strife, disagreement, frustration, and even embitterment. Of the 97 supervisors who took the course, 19 left the company and another 25 sought other positions. Of those who had contact with top management, 80 percent became dissatisfied. 83 percent of those who took the course said it was a failure because it did not change *top management* attitudes! The dissatisfied group (those who either left the company or sought other employment) included nearly all the best qualified and most intelligent of the supervisors.[24]

The important thing about evaluation is not to seek perfection, but to ask the right questions. Here are the important ones.

## Management Training Policies

Is there a training policy?

Is it expressed in writing?

Is the training policy properly integrated with the over-all personnel policy?

How was the policy prepared?

Is it well communicated, understood, and accepted?

Is it imaginative and comprehensive?

Is there a definite plan for the training of management staff at all levels?

Does the plan make provision for systematic and continuous needs analysis

- providing for future needs as well as current needs and problems?
- supporting procedures and facilities to ensure that the plan is implemented?
- controlling and evaluating on a regular basis?

Should the management's training objectives, the scope of the policies, and the overall plan be changed?

Is the training provided really essential?

Is the training focused on the highest priorities?

Are there significant gaps in the training plan?

## Management Training and Organizations

Are the responsibilities for results in management training clearly defined and understood? Is there a satisfactory contribution by staff, specialists, and executive management?

If there is a specialized management training organization, does it fit, in a balanced way, into the overall organization and particularly into the personnel function?

Is the attitude of executive management toward training constructive? Does the training organization counsel on or help to provide

- induction training?
- basic job training?
- refresher training, keeping up to date?
- training on advanced levels, or geared to promotion at all levels?

Does the training organization contribute to
- individual development?
- group development?

Does the training organization ensure that the scope of training (e.g., top management, supervision, technical, administrative) is satisfactory?

If there are specialists on the training staff, are they professionally competent?

If there are training facilities (e.g., lecture training rooms), are equipment, location, space, seating, heating, ventilation, and room layout satisfactory?

Is there a budget for management training and proper control over it and the results which it should achieve?

Should the organization of management training be altered?

Should the special training staff be decreased or increased in numbers, improved in quality, or otherwise changed?

Could training facilities be improved?

### Training Courses—Contents and Methods

What are the objectives of each course?

How were these objectives determined?

How were these subjects and these emphases determined?

How relevant are the subjects to the trainees' actual needs, interests, and capacities?

What training methods (lecture, lesson, discussion,

films, film strips, transparencies, blackboards, flannel board, etc.) are used?

How well are these aids used and how appropriate are they?

How effective are these methods (skill of instructor, questioning technique, etc.)?

What notes are provided?

Are the physical accommodations satisfactory?

How many people attend? Have attended? Still are eligible to attend?

What tests or checks are there to ensure that knowledge or skills have been acquired?

What follow-up to the training is there?

Does the course in this form provide a useful purpose?

What changes, if any, should there be in its content, presentation, etc., in order to improve it?

### Results of Training Courses

To what extent were the objectives of the course achieved?

What *evidence* is there of
- measurable improvement in results?
- active use of knowledge and skills?
- new attitudes?
- better relationships?
- reduced turnover?

To what extent did management training resolve the problems it was designed to resolve?

If the change was not achieved, why not? (Selection of people, poor needs analysis, bad instruction, faulty course construction, inadequate follow-up and encouragement, and so forth.)

Did it produce changes which were not planned? If so, were these good or bad?

What training is now needed to further improve performance against present job requirements?

## Salaries and Succession Plans

The manager's need to be rewarded according to his contribution means that the company must have a progressive salary policy and plan for succession. A salary structure should:

- ☐ Reward managers equitably in relation to each other, their subordinates, and their personal contribution to the business.
- ☐ Provide an incentive to better performance rather than merely reward past services.
- ☐ Be more or less commensurate with those offered by other companies in the same geographical location for jobs in the same category.
- ☐ Be flexible in operation, not mechanistic and bureaucratic.

In addition to salaries, a *progressive* approach to fringe benefits—vacations, pensions, cars, share options, and so on—is necessary. The growth of management placement agencies has been healthy in bringing out into the open going rates and general market conditions.

Economic rewards are important, but the knowledge that there is a systematic approach to selection and succession within a company is also influential in building high morale. Over-preoccupation with promotion is frustrating and the company must have a plan for:

It is important to take stock regularly of the present group of managers—their experience, abilities, and interests—and to see how well they are performing in their present jobs.

It is a surprising fact that many companies do not have up-to-date information on their managers in a convenient form for planning purposes. How can even a simple retirement schedule be compiled without age records? If the "qualifications and experience" of managers are not on record, the company is more likely to make inadequate use of its human resources.

Some indication of the man's personal ambitions and interests is also helpful. One company, which had been quietly planning the next step for a bright young operations research manager into general management, was dismayed when he said "I don't want to be a general manager. My ambition is to head up OR in this group ultimately."

### SUCCESSION PLAN

Succession planning needs to relate the individual to the organization needs. This must be planned in depth, since every move has a buffer impact up and down the line and sometimes sideways. The selection methods must be effective to support the plan.

### CAREER PLANNING

The experience of managers can be arranged so that they acquire the knowledge and skills for future posts which they might hold.

Succession planning can never be perfect. People leave unexpectedly, the "high flier" reaches a plateau prematurely, and organization needs are changed by outside influences. However, it is just as necessary to have a five-year, two-year, and next-year plan in management manpower planning as it is for finance and markets. The failure to do this can be very serious because the lead time required to build up a team of young men is perhaps on the order of ten years. Crash recruitment programs forced on the company by an apparent shortage of talent within can damage the morale of existing managers. One benefit of an MBO program is that it compels the *present* group of managers to recognize the scale and nature of forward manager manpower needs.

A very small company has less need for forms or procedures. Indeed it may have to be faced frankly that succession may *invariably* mean bringing in a qualified man from outside.

Medium-size companies must have some formality and discipline if succession is to be well organized. Some use an organization chart type of presentation (Exhibit 24) and others a column type of presentation (Exhibit 25).

Large companies often delegate succession planning to divisions and subsidiaries, with the center maintaining responsibility for the succession at very senior levels. The center may also hold onto career planning for "high fliers" throughout the company and advise on the principles of good succession planning without necessarily imposing a single set of techniques.

*Exhibit 24.* Succession plan, organization chart type.

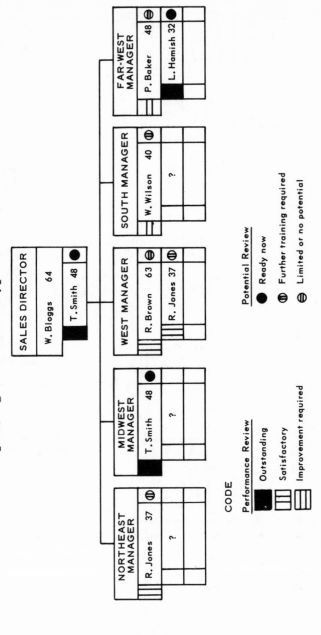

| SALES DIRECTOR | |
|---|---|
| W. Bloggs | 64 |
| T. Smith | 48 ● |

| NORTHEAST MANAGER | |
|---|---|
| R. Jones | 37 ⊕ |
| ? | |

| MIDWEST MANAGER | |
|---|---|
| T. Smith | 48 ● |
| ? | |

| WEST MANAGER | |
|---|---|
| R. Brown | 63 ⊕ |
| R. Jones | 37 ⊕ |

| SOUTH MANAGER | |
|---|---|
| W. Wilson | 40 ⊕ |
| ? | |

| FAR-WEST MANAGER | |
|---|---|
| P. Baker | 48 ⊕ |
| L. Hamish | 32 ● |

CODE

**Performance Review**

■ Outstanding

▤ Satisfactory

▥ Improvement required

**Potential Review**

● Ready now

⊕ Further training required

⊖ Limited or no potential

*Exhibit 25.* Succession plan, column listing.

COMPANY : X
DIVISION : Y
DEPARTMENT : Z
DATE :

| Job Title | Present Job-holder | Estimated Date of Leaving and Reason, e.g., Retirement | Immediate Successor | Age | Company Service | Present Job | Service in Present Job | Performance Rating | Readiness | Training and Experience Required |
|-----------|--------------------|--------------------------------------------------------|---------------------|-----|-----------------|-------------|------------------------|--------------------|-----------|----------------------------------|
|           |                    |                                                        |                     |     |                 |             |                        |                    |           |                                  |

## Organization and Control

The introduction of management by objectives into a company will always challenge the effectiveness of the organization structure and the pattern of control information.

### ORGANIZATION PLANNING

Key Results Analysis is an effective means of diagnosing organizational problems. The link between organization structure and MBO is particularly important because the analysis of individual jobs makes sense only in the broader picture of the business structure. One management job has to be understood in relation to others. This is well summarized in the "Objectives of the Glacier Project" where it is stated,

> . . . managerial effectiveness is partly a function of the personality and character of the manager. Training can do little to change these personal qualities.
>
> A manager's behavior is, however, strongly influenced by the correctness of definition of the role he occupies, the relationship of this role to other roles and the total system, the terms of reference governing his role, and the degrees to which the manager understands these matters. Modification and clarification of such conditions can, therefore, produce significant changes in managerial behavior and effectiveness.[25]

A badly designed organization structure presents obstacles to high performance, no matter how hard-working and able the managers are. A survey by The Conference Board of 167 United States companies refers to the

. . . increasingly close association of management development and organization planning. In many situations, these responsibilities are combined in one company unit: development is one of the responsibilities assigned to the organization planning unit; or, less commonly, organization planning is assigned to the management development staff. These responsibilities are recognized as the two sides of one coin.[26]

With the rich understanding that emerges from the Key Results Analysis about how an organization is operating and the difficulties being experienced, the present structure can be critically reviewed. Here are some useful questions to ask toward that end.

*Does the organization provide for proper use of human resources?*
> Are managers doing tasks which should be delegated?
>
> Are managers doing tasks which should be done by machine?
>
> Are jobs too "small," so that people can't grow?
>
> Are jobs too "big," so that they are done inefficiently?
>
> Is there too much "insurance" built into the organization—advisers, technical and specialist support, etc.—so that the managers and supervisors really do not have a management job left?
>
> Is the time spent in a job too long, so that people get stale?
>
> Or so short that they never really master the job before they leave?

*Is there an effective division of work to be done?*
> Is the basic division between functions sound?
>
> Is there confusion between staff and line?

What is the balance of power between HQ and the individual units? Is it sound?

Is there proper provision for policy making as an activity separate from execution?

*Are responsibilities and objectives really understood?*

Did Key Results Analysis show that managers really knew the results they were expected to achieve?

Did it show that they could distinguish between important and unimportant elements in their work?

Do managers understand the roles of others with whom they have a working relationship?

*Is there a sound line of command?*

Is there a clear line of direct authority from top to bottom?

Do functional links confuse or strengthen this?

How many management levels are there?

What is the span of control? Is it sound?

*Is there provision for control and accountability?*

Is there good control over Key Results Areas?

Are there gaps?

Is there a sound pattern of reporting, written and oral?

Are controls at a frequency and in a form which help good decision making? Or do they impede it?

What sort of decisions do managers themselves make?

How important are these decisions?

Do they have an impact beyond their own job?

What is the time span before someone checks up on the decision?

*Is the structure working in good spirit?*
>Is there a sense of collaboration in getting things done?
>
>Is the structure reasonably well understood and accepted?
>
>Is it flexible and commonsensical in daily practice?
>Or is it rigid and confusing?
>
>Does it encourage delay and politics through lack of clarity?

### CONTROL INFORMATION

Unless a manager can measure to what extent he is succeeding and where special attention should be focused to overcome obstacles, it is impossible for him to perform well.

The vital priority is to establish control over the key results of his job. This can lead to a reduction of paperwork as information about unimportant matters is discontinued, but its real value is in creating a new attitude of mind. As Drucker writes,

>The real difficulty lies indeed not in determining what objectives we need, but in deciding how to set them. There is only one fruitful way to make this decision: by determining what shall be measured in each area and what the yardstick of measurement should be. *For the measurement used determines what one pays attention to.* It makes things visible and tangible. The things included in the measurement become relevant; the things omitted are out of sight and out of mind.[27] (Italics added.)

The form and frequency of information are also important. Too much information can paralyze action;

too little can create dangerous ignorance. A systematic analysis is required, starting with the needs of the individual manager. This ensures that management control information is not viewed only in financial accounting terms, but embraces all the important factors, internal and external, which must be understood in order to check results against planned objectives, encourage better setting of objectives, shape alternative solutions and strategies, and make better decisions.

Starting at the manager level also ensures that the timing, choice of measuring method, and form of presentation can be made to suit his needs rather than those of the professional accountant. It has an integrating influence on different sources of information.

The problem of measurement is one of the most complex in this broad subject of improving management performance. A great deal of interest and research is apparent as top management seeks to measure better what it knows to be critical. Ralph Cordiner of General Electric wrote,

> It is an immense problem to organize and communicate the information required to operate a large, decentralized organization. . . . What is required . . . is . . . a penetrating and orderly study of the business in its entirety to discover what specific information is needed at each particular position in view of the decisions to be made there.[28]

The late Stanley F. Teele, dean of the Harvard Business School, supported this view when he said,

> I think the capacity to manage knowledge will be still more important to the manager. . . . The manager will need to increase his skill in deciding what knowledge he needs.[29]

130

Some of the practical problems we are currently meeting in our consulting practice are:

- [ ] The continued use of a static information pattern when the business is itself changing rapidly, for example, through decentralization, growth, diversification, new technology.
- [ ] Uncertainty about the cost of securing information in relation to the potential benefits it will bring.
- [ ] A narrow view of control—for example, the absence of control data about the market environment in which the business operates.
- [ ] "Technical" problems of measurement. Encouraging progress is being made as we learn to make better use of electronic data processing.

Operational research methods also help by providing a more rigorous mathematical solution to information difficulties. In the years ahead the managers in the large groups may be helped by a specialist in information technology. Recent experiments in the use of network analysis techniques in analyzing information have been encouraging.[30]

Better management performance depends greatly on our capacity to measure and inform, so that self-control can be exercised by the individual, particularly in relation to his key results. Many years ago Lord Kelvin presented a similar challenge:

> When you can measure what you are speaking about, and express it in numbers, you know something about it. But when you cannot measure it, when you cannot express it in numbers, your knowledge is of a meager and unsatisfactory kind.[31]

# Wider Implications

Sound techniques, properly integrated and supported by a framework of company policy, contribute greatly to success, but this total approach to management by objectives is a wider, more searching, and more rewarding way of managing a business.

Although a great deal has yet to be developed and improved, it may be useful to highlight some general points:

1. Lasting success depends primarily on the interest and attitude of mind of the chief executive. It is he who must think through the objectives of the business and provide the practical facilities for them to be achieved. He must develop a genuine sense of participation among his managers and be receptive to their constructive criticism. He must concentrate on accomplishment rather than promotion and be willing to delegate responsibility and encourage risk taking. Small wonder that some chief executives prefer more traditional and less demanding approaches to the development of their managers.

2. It follows that every manager has a dual responsibility: to develop himself, and to create a demanding environment which will stimulate the self-development of his subordinates. The span of executive command is the span of direct personal responsibility for subordinate growth.

3. There must be a sustained effort to clarify objectives for the company and to reconcile with these the personal (job and emotional) goals of individual managers. This unified sense of purpose within a business, concentrated on what really matters, can be a

formidable tool of profit improvement and cost reduction.

4. The deep involvement of managers, individually and in groups, in defining key results, securing change, and reviewing success is fundamental to the MBO approach. This underlines again that self-development is the way to unleash the contribution and enthusiasm of managers. It gives practical support to the view of the late Douglas McGregor that

> The expenditure of physical and mental effort in work is as natural as play or rest.
>
> External control and the threat of punishment are not the only means for bringing about effort toward organizational objectives.
>
> Man will exercise self-control in the service to which he is committed. Commitment to objectives is dependent on the rewards associated with their achievement. The most important rewards are those that satisfy needs for self-respect and personal improvement.
>
> The average human being learns, under proper conditions, not only to accept but to seek responsibility.
>
> The capacity to exercise a relatively high degree of imagination, ingenuity, and creativity in the solution of organizational problems is widely, not narrowly, distributed in the population.
>
> Under the conditions of modern industrial life, the intellectual potentialities of the average human being are only partially utilized.[32]

5. The approach is focused on results. It is concerned with *measurable* benefits for manager and company, not with vague generalization and platitude. Thus, it is not enough to agree on what a man must do, but also on what he must achieve; not enough to analyze

a problem, but also to produce an action plan to begin to solve it; not enough to issue instructions, but also to associate with them measures of accountability.

Management by objectives is dynamic in philosophy, looking at tomorrow's opportunities rather than yesterday's mistakes. It follows that forms and procedures are not sacred. Flexibility in ensuring that the company's human, physical, and financial resources are concentrated in the areas of greatest opportunity is dominant. It may be thought that this insistence on measurable results will arouse antagonism in managers, since its sharpness could make them more vulnerable to criticism. The opposite is true in practice. Managers wish to be judged fairly according to an established set of standards, for as William Whyte wrote,

> No one likes to be played checkers with, and the man The Organization needs most is precisely the man who is most sensitive on this point. To control one's destiny and not be controlled by it; to know which way the path will fork and to make the turning oneself; *to have some index of achievement that no one can dispute—concrete and tangible for all to see, not dependent on the attitude of others.* It is an independence he will never have in full measure but he must forever seek it.[33] (Italics added.)

6. The concern with results shifts the emphasis from personality factors and personal style in management to achievements. It is the middle road between the view of a human being as just another machine and the extremist school of "Human Relations" which emphasized social factors to the detriment of technical and economic factors in business.

7. The improvement of performance and people is regarded as a continuing process, for the business and all its managers, not a shot-in-the-arm program for a chosen few.

8. Imaginative and broadly conceived policy statements can be helpful in knitting together these various techniques into a coherent pattern.

Such a policy must be tailor-made for the company concerned, since the discussions about its content are as important as the final statement. For example, General Electric's policy in relation to management development, as stated as long ago as 1955,[34] is

- To provide all managers and potential managers with challenges and opportunities for maximum self-development on their present jobs and for advancement as earned.
- To work toward improving skill and competence throughout the entire manager group so as to help General Electric managers to become equal to the demands of *tomorrow's* management job.
- To operate to furnish the company with both the number and kind of managers that will be needed in the years ahead.
- To encourage systematic habits and procedures to make it simpler for each manager to discharge his manager development responsibility.

9. We should take to heart L. F. Urwick's warning that a business cannot solve its problems merely by buying a technique or system: "Every business enterprise is a living organism, with its own traditions, its own climate of opinion, its own special make-up. Every situation is different. And every kind of system has to be custom-built to the individual business." [35]

This is extremely important when considering the relevance of management by objectives to smaller companies. Everything said in principle in this book applies to these companies: no business is too small to have clear-cut objectives, job clarity, performance and potential review, and training and development. To use blindly the detailed techniques and procedures developed in large companies would be absurd. Within the basic principles a vast variety of methods, formal and informal, can be tailor-made to suit particular circumstances.

### CONCLUSION

MBO is not a perfected package deal and there are unresolved problems. How can we measure precisely long-term R&D objectives? How is management potential identified at an early stage? Nevertheless, encouraging progress has been made in creating a set of proven methods which together make a total and comprehensible management system to improve company and manager performance. The "scientific" managers and the behavioral and social scientists have gone a long way toward reconciling their viewpoints and practices, and business planning is being integrated with the creative self-development of human beings.

Every manager can improve his performance and job satisfaction through a positive approach to management by objectives.

*Part Three*

---

# IMPROVEMENT
# ANALYSIS
# CHECKLIST

## Performance

Are you satisfied with the results being achieved now by your company/department/section?

In what areas is there clearly scope for improved performance of the business? Of the managers?

Are you sure that precious high-quality resources are not drifting into low-opportunity areas?

How does your performance compare with that of your best competitors?

## Objectives

Do you have clear and specific objectives for your company/department/section?

Do they look beyond next year?

What is the range of objectives?

For example, are manager performance, labor relations, and innovation objectives included?

Did your subordinate managers contribute to these objectives?

Did they understand them thoroughly?

Are they really committed to achieving them?

## Policies

Do you have policy statements in the important areas of the business to provide guidance on recurring questions? Are minor decisions frequently referred upward for policy clearance?

## Manager Results

Is each manager really clear about

the key results he must achieve?

the performance standards and criteria by which he will be judged?

the control information he receives in order to monitor progress?

the limits of his authority?

If you have job descriptions already, can you be sure they are used as a *management tool?* Or were they prepared as an "interesting exercise," now filed and forgotten?

Were they imposed, or did managers make a genuine contribution to their job descriptions?

Does each manager have an agreed plan, with standards and time schedules, to improve his performance?

Are jobs big and demanding enough to provide growth opportunities for men?

## *Organization*

Is there a sound division of work to be done?
> Is the scope of your company (division, department) great enough to warrant decentralization?
> Does the scope of responsibilities warrant delegation?
> Is there confusion about the responsibilities of staff/line?
> Should the overall organization structure be functional or by product? Geographical?
> Are any functions not covered?

Is there a clear line of command?

How many managerial levels are there from managing director to first-line supervisor? Is this too many?

Are there too many "small" jobs and not enough that stretch people?

Is the organization working in good spirit?
> Do people have a sense of collaboration?
> Is management flexible about rules?
> Is the atmosphere colored by power politics?
> Are people preoccupied with status?

## *Communication*

Do managers listen as much as they talk?

Is there a flow of information down the line so that the sense of common purpose is built up?

State your personal feelings:

> Are standards and controls used mainly as tools of self-help or as "threats" from above?
>
> Do you feel free to approach your boss with ideas and suggestions for change?
>
> Does your boss consult you on problems not strictly within your responsibility?
>
> Do you receive enough information—written and verbal—to know how you're getting on and how the business is progressing overall?
>
> Are mistakes generally treated as "crimes" or as opportunities to learn?
>
> Do you feel you are *over*-managed?
>
> Does your boss help, train, and guide you on the job, or do you "just pick it up"?
>
> To what extent do you feel you're working on your own? Cooperating with others as a team member?

## Control

Do managers have control information on all key results they must achieve?

Is the information simple? Relevant? Timely? Acceptable? A good basis for self-control?

When did you last make a critical study of the information and control systems and paper work?

Is there too *much* information?

Is it costing too much?

Do managers believe that the financial budget is synonymous with their objectives?

## Use of Time

Would you say managers make good use of their time?

Do they have a knowledge of priorities so that time can be concentrated on important issues?

Are there too many meetings and committees where one manager could get the result better alone? Or where the chairman's skill is inadequate to guide the group?

Do managers delegate sufficiently so that they have time to concentrate on the things only they can do well?


## Management Development

### Training

Do you prepare a training plan for your managers? Who creates it—executive management, staff management, or both?

If you run internal management courses, how do you identify the need for this? How do you evaluate the benefits of the course?

Think of the last training course or seminar you attended personally.

> Was it useful?
>
> Did you make any action proposals on your return?
>
> Have you made direct use of what you learned?

### Review

Do you have a regular manager performance and potential review scheme?

If not, how do you judge and record your managers' performance and potential?

Does your scheme focus on the *results* a manager achieves or on "the kind of man he is" or on "what he does"?

What practical use do you make of reviews? For example, when did you last identify and give accelerated promotion to an outstanding man? When did you last remove a man who could or would not meet the minimum job standards?

*Succession*

Do you have a company succession plan?

Do top managers take time to discuss both promising young men and those who present some problems?

Is it difficult to fill key management posts when they become vacant?

Are you hoarding talent which could—in the interests of the man and company—be better used elsewhere?

*Rewards*

Does your salary system attract and hold the right quality and number of managers?

Does it reward managers in relation to (1) the results they achieve and (2) their potential?

# REFERENCES

## Part One

1. International MBO Conference, British Institute of Management (London, December 1970).
2. Peter Drucker, *The Practice of Management* (New York: Harper & Row, 1954).
3. Harry Levinson, "Management by Whose Objectives?" *Harvard Business Review* (July–August 1970), p. 125.
4. George S. Odiorne, *Training by Objectives* (London: Macmillan, 1970).
5. Peter Drucker, *The Age of Discontinuity* (New York: Harper & Row, 1969).
6. G. J. Perkins, "Accounting by Objectives," *Management* (Irish Institute of Management, November 1968).
7. P. J. Chartrand, "Measuring the Change Process," *Management by Objectives Journal,* London, Vol. 1, No. 4 (May 1972).
8. Eric Goddard, "Developing MBO Within the Greater London Council," *Management by Objectives Journal,* London, Vol. 1, No. 1 (July 1971).
9. Sister Rosemary Miller, "Living by Objectives," *Management by Objectives Journal,* London, Vol. 1, No. 2 (October 1971).

## Part Two

1. Robert J. House, *California Management Review* (Spring 1965).
2. Douglas McGregor, *The Human Side of Enterprise* (New York: McGraw-Hill, 1960).
3. Moorhead Wright, "How to Foster Individual Growth," *The Supervisor* (November 1961), pp. 9–11.
4. George A. Steiner, *Top Management Planning* (New York: Macmillan, 1969).
5. Harold Stieglitz, *The Chief Executive—and His Job* (New York: The Conference Board, 1969).
6. Unpublished.
7. Douglas McGregor, *The Professional Manager* (New York: McGraw-Hill, 1967).
8. See also "The Task Force in Management by Objectives" in John Humble, ed., *Management by Objectives in Action* (New York: McGraw-Hill, 1970).
9. R. J. Wills, "Performance Improvement in Manufacturing Management" (Society of Manufacturing Engineers, 1971).
10. Robert F. Bales, *Interaction Process Analysis* (Philadelphia: Lansdowne Press, 1971).
11. Douglas McGregor, *The Professional Manager* (New York: McGraw-Hill, 1967).
12. Charles H. Granger, "The Hierarchy of Objectives," *Harvard Business Review* (May–June 1964), pp. 63–74.
13. Robert H. Schaffer, *Managing by Total Objectives*, AMA Management Bulletin 52 (1964).
14. Wilfred Brown, "What Is Work?" *Harvard Business Review* (September–October 1962), pp. 121–129.

15. N. F. Maier, *Superior-Subordinate Communication in Management*, AMA Research Study 52 (1961).
16. Peter F. Drucker, "Managing for Business Effectiveness," *Harvard Business Review* (May–June 1963), pp. 53–60.
17. Kay H. Rowe, "An Appraisal of Appraisals," *Journal of Management Studies*, Vol. 1, No. 1 (March 1964), pp. 1–25.
18. Robert L. Miles, "Evaluating Results Against Objectives," *Management Record* (July–August 1962), pp. 39–44.
19. Douglas McGregor, "An Uneasy Look at Performance Appraisal," *Harvard Business Review* (May–June 1957), pp. 89–95.
20. Kay H. Rowe, op. cit., p. 14.
21. Rensis Likert "Motivational Approach to Management," *Harvard Business Review* (July–August 1959), pp. 75–82.
22. Marion S. Kellogg, "Performance Appraisal and Training," *Journal of the American Society of Training Directors* (July 1962), pp. 19–24.
23. England, April 1971.
24. A. J. M. Sykes, "The Effect of a Supervisory Training Course in Changing Supervisors' Perceptions and Expectations of the Role of Management," *Human Relations*, Vol. 15, No. 3 (August 1962), pp. 227–243.
25. Unpublished source. But see Elliott Jaques, *The Changing Culture of a Factory* (New York: The Dryden Press, 1952).
26. *Developing Managerial Competence: Changing Concepts, Emerging Practices*, Studies in Personnel Policy No. 189 (New York: The Conference Board, 1964).

27. Peter F. Drucker, *The Practice of Management* (New York: Harper & Row, 1954), p. 64.
28. Ralph J. Cordiner, *New Frontiers for Professional Managers* (New York: McGraw-Hill, 1956).
29. Stanley F. Teele, "Your Job and Mine—What Change Is Doing to Them," *Harvard Business School Bulletin* (August 1960), pp. 7–14.
30. Norbert Stahl, "Information Networking," *Mechanical Engineering* (December 1964), pp. 35–37.
31. Sir William Thomson, First Baron Kelvin, "Electrical Units of Measurement," *Popular Lectures and Addresses*, 2d ed., Vol. 1 (London: Macmillan, 1891), pp. 80–143.
32. Douglas McGregor, *The Human Side of Enterprise* (New York: McGraw-Hill, 1960).
33. William H. Whyte, Jr., *The Organization Man* (New York: Simon & Schuster, 1956), p. 167.
34. Harold F. Smiddy, "General Electric's Philosophy and Approach for Manager Development," in *Fitting Management Development to Company Needs*, AMA General Management Series No. 174 (1955).
35. L. F. Urwick, *The Pattern of Management* (London: Pitman, 1956).

# FURTHER READING

In addition to the sources already given in the references, the following list is recommended.

Ansoff, H. Igor, *Corporate Strategy: An Analytical Approach to Business Policy for Growth and Expansion*. New York: McGraw-Hill, 1965.

Drucker, Peter F., *Managing for Results*. New York: Harper & Row, 1964.

Drucker, Peter F., *The Effective Executive*. New York: Harper & Row, 1967.

Mali, Paul, *Managing by Objectives*. New York: Wiley, 1972.

Miller, Ernest C., *Objectives and Standards: An Approach to Planning and Control*. AMA Research Study 74, 1966.

Morrisey, George L., *Management by Objectives and Results*. Reading, Mass.: Addison-Wesley, 1970.

Morrisey, George L., *Appraisal and Development Through Objectives and Results*. Reading, Mass.: Addison-Wesley, 1972.

National Industrial Conference Board, *Managing by and with Objectives*. Personnel Policy 212. New York: NICB, 1968.

Odiorne, George S., *Management by Objectives: A System of Managerial Leadership*. New York: Pitman, 1965.

Reddin, W. J., *Effective Management by Objectives: The 3-D Method of MBO*. New York: McGraw-Hill, 1971.

# FILMS ON MBO

By John Humble. Available through BNA Films, Rock-
ville, Md.

> *Colt: A Case History*
> *Defining the Manager's Job*
> *Focus the Future*
> *Management by Objectives*
> *Management Training*
> *Performance and Potential Review*